MODERN NOVELISTS

General Editor: Norman Page

MODERN NOVELISTS

MODERN NOVELISTS

V. S. NAIPAUL

Bruce King

St. Martin's Press   New York

First published in the United States of America in 1993

Printed in Hong Kong

ISBN 0–312–08646–6

Library of Congress Cataloging-in-Publication Data
King, Bruce, 1933–
  V. S. Naipaul/Bruce King.
  p.   cm. — (Modern novelists.)
  Includes bibliographical references and index.
  ISBN 0–312–08646–6
  1. Naipaul, V. S. (Vidiadhar Surajprasad), 1932–   —Criticism and
  interpretation.   I. Title.   II. Series.
  PR9272.9.N32Z749   1993
  832'.914—dc20   92–21012
                                                            CIP

Contents

To Cheryl and Michael

and

Lisa and Philippe

General Editor's Preface

The death of the novel has often been announced, and part of the secret of its obstinate vitality must be its capacity for growth, adaptation, self-renewal and self-transformation: like some vigorous organism in a speeded-up Darwinian ecosystem, it adapts itself quickly to a changing world. War and revolution, economic crisis and social change, radically new ideologies such as Marxism and Freudianism, have made this century unprecedented in human history in the speed and extent of change, but the novel has shown an extraordinary capacity to find new forms and techniques and to accommodate new ideas and conceptions of human nature and human experience, and even to take up new positions on the nature of fiction itself.

In the generations immediately preceding and following 1914, the novel underwent a radical redefinition of its nature and possibilities. The present series of monographs is devoted to the novelists who created the modern novel and to those who, in their turn, either continued and extended, or reacted against and rejected, the traditions established during that period of intense exploration and experiment. It includes a number of those who lived and wrote in the nineteenth century but whose innovative contribution to the art of fiction makes it impossible to ignore them in any account of the origins of the modern novel; it also includes the so-called 'modernists' and those who in the mid- and late twentieth century have emerged as outstanding practitioners of this genre. The scope is, inevitably, international; not only, in the migratory and exile-haunted world of our century, do writers refuse to heed national frontiers – 'English' literature lays claim to Conrad the Pole, Henry James the American, and Joyce the Irishman – but geniuses such as Flaubert, Dostoevsky and Kafka have had an influence on the fiction of many nations.

Each volume in the series is intended to provide an introduction to the fiction of the writer concerned, both for those approaching him or her for the first time and for those who are already familiar with some parts of the achievement in question and now wish to place it in the context of the total *oeuvre*. Although essential information relating to the writer's life and times is given, usually in an opening chapter, the approach is primarily critical and the emphasis is not upon 'background' or generalisations but upon close examination of important texts. Where an author is notably prolific, major texts have been made to convey, more summarily, a sense of the nature and quality of the author's work as a whole. Those who want to read further will find suggestions in the select bibliography included in each volume. Many novelists are, of course, not only novelists but also poets, essayists, biographers, dramatists, travel writers and so forth; many have practised shorter forms of fiction; and many have written letters or kept diaries that constitute a significant part of their literary output. A brief study cannot hope to deal with all these in detail, but where the shorter fiction and the non-fictional writings, public and private, have an important relationship to the novels, some space has been devoted to them.

NORMAN PAGE

1
Introduction

V. S. Naipaul, one of the most original, controversial and best writers of our time, was born in an impoverished rural, Hindi-speaking area of Trinidad. By the time Naipaul was fourteen years old he had made up his mind to leave Trinidad as soon as he could. His father, a local journalist, introduced him to serious literature and instilled in him the notion that he should become a writer. A hard-earned scholarship to Oxford University brought him to England where he has lived, written more than twenty books, won many literary prizes and in 1990 was knighted for his services to English literature.

Naipaul's career and achievement can be seen as part of the worldwide cultural changes that resulted in such important writers as Chinua Achebe, Wole Soyinka, Nadine Gordimer, Derek Walcott, Margaret Atwood, Michael Ondaatje, Salman Rushdie and, more recently, Ben Okri, Timothy Mo and Kazuo Ishiguro. He was part of a generation that had to face the problems that resulted from the withdrawal of imperial order and the resulting cultural confusion. Yet his story is perhaps unique in his having started with so little and having come so far. Because of family and Trinidadian circumstances he is an expatriate who, starting with no other means than his will and the talents that he has developed through hard work, has supported himself as a writer. Although he claims that writing does not come easily to him, except during a few very brief periods he has had no other employment. For his first twenty years in England he never felt at home and is still aware of himself as an outsider.

Being from the Asian Indian minority in black-dominated Trinidad his perspective on decolonization, imperialism, black–white relations and other themes of post-colonial literatures is more complicated than that of nationalists and their foreign sympathiz-

1

ers. He regards himself as a former colonial who has become a homeless cosmopolitan. As his writing has become more familiar and as he has revealed more about himself and his past, he can be seen as having projected much of his personal experience on his analysis of the contemporary world; yet while unique his experience is representative of the major social, psychological, political and cultural changes of our time. His views often have the effect of paradox and surprise forcing a re-examination of received opinions. He objects that describing him as a West Indian writer is patronizing and limiting. A severe critic of India and the shortcomings of the newly independent nations, he is also a nationalist who feels humiliated by the weakness and exploitation of the colonized; he blames European imperialism for the problems it left its former colonies, while praising it for bringing peace and modern thought to areas of the world that remained medieval and debilitated by continual local wars. There is a moral honesty in his work, a refusal to sentimentalize England or the former colonies.

Naipaul has a sense of vocation as a writer and needs to be understood as a writer before being seen in other contexts. His books are written and revised over many years as he tries to find the right form and selection of events for the idea. He has an unusually precise command of the English language, of its various registers, and is fascinated by regional, technical and amusing uses. He is concerned with the need for continuity, tension and liveliness in his sentences, paragraphs, scenes and chapters. While he is exact and economical in his descriptions, with an eye for details of landscapes, his often otherwise objective prose is poetic in its rich patterns of sound, cadence, rhythm and rhetorical devices. The prose is varied, energetic, filled with ironies, echoes, parodies and allusions. It reads well aloud. His deceptively prosaic, stripped-down manner is supported by alliterations, repeated words and phrases. Many of his central characters are unlikable and narrate their story in a manner that is revealing yet attractive. In the later novels, the dry, but hilariously amusing, comedy of the dialogue and the nuances of what the narrator is saying might be missed by the reader carried along by the movement of the prose; reading aloud helps focus attention on what is being shown and implied. While there are four recognizable periods of Naipaul's work, characterized by differences in subject matter, manner, technique and complexity, there is a continuity of concerns, themes and certain formal structures in his novels and books of travel.

For someone of East Indian descent in Trinidad to have decided early in life that he wanted to become a writer and to have kept to such a decision, although there was and still is no market for serious literature capable of supporting a writer in the Caribbean, is quixotic and brave. Few authors from the colonies had previously supported themselves as serious writers. Naipaul lived for many years the hand-to-mouth existence of an aspiring writer in London, where there was a literary market, but before 'post-colonial' and 'multicultural' were fashionable terms. After he had become highly regarded by literary critics and a winner of many literary prizes, his royalties from books remained small and he had few North American readers. Eventually he found an additional source of income in travelling to and reporting on the social and cultural problems of other parts of the world, especially the newly independent nations.

Such travel corresponded with Naipaul's own need to find new subject matter beyond his memories of Trinidad and provided him with a more interesting life than the solitary existence of a novelist; it contributed to his awareness of the wider world. His own experience first in Trinidad, then as an expatriate in England and later as an unsettled ex-colonial always on the move between countries, replicates the restlessness, dissatisfactions, migrations of people and rapid social and cultural changes of the present world. The more he wrote about the modern world and tried to analyse it the more important he regarded his travel books and essays, with the result that literary genres began to blur, mix and blend; he created new forms in such books as *In a Free State* and *The Enigma of Arrival* that combined autobiography, travel writing, analysis and fiction. The act of writing, and his methods of finding material and the proper form, also became his subject matter.

Naipaul's fiction often has subtexts: the novels can be understood as autobiographical in the sense that they are projections of his own life and anxieties of homelessness, of living in more than one culture, of needing to find a narrative order for experience, of needing to achieve, of needing to create, of having to build a monument to his own existence through his writing. His fiction is also often based on models to which he alludes. Such intertextuality provides a sense of historical continuity, revision and renewal.[1] His books are also filled with characters who write, want to write or pretend to write; they are filled with parodies of bad writing, people who out of ignorance confuse serious literature with letter

writing, bad journalism, pamphlets, unedited diaries, pornographic
fantasies. There are characters who mistake prominence in the
cultural industry, broadcasting or occasional book reviewing, with
being a writer. Because Naipaul is interested in historical writing
and sees himself as an historian of his time, someone inquiring
into the condition of society and culture in the late and post-
colonial era, there are many bad, foolish or mistaken historians in
his novels. He has been writing a history of our time, a record and
analysis of many of the main events, such as decolonization in
India, Africa and the Caribbean, the growing conflict between
Islamic religious fundamentalism and Western enlightenment, or
racial relations in the southern United States after the victory of
the civil rights movement. He has often returned to the same
places, India, Africa, the Caribbean, England, noting changes, re-
examining society, revising his analysis. His novels are usually
based on fact, known people and events.[2] The travel books are
filled with characters, voices, representative documents, places.
Naipaul has created an image of our era and its discontents.

He has made conscious decisions about his subject matter or the
direction his writing should take. They were decisions made from
analysing his own situation as an expatriate West Indian writing for
the British or, later, American literary market. He has also made
decisions that can be explained by his own obsessions and by the
high seriousness with which he invests being a writer. Much effort
went into research for *The Loss of El Dorado*, an attempt to understand the historical causes that led to the creation and problems of
modern Trinidad.

Although Naipaul has published a book on the average of every
eighteen months, his novels and many of his non-fictional works
are often over a period of years written, revised, left unfinished
and then started again from the beginning. There is the need to
find the right 'idea', a story – selected from some larger experience – which will embody the themes; the 'idea' includes such
methods of presentation and embodiment of the idea as the structure of the book, the kind and treatment of the narrator, the
language of narration, the recurring images, the tonalities. Each
Naipaul novel is a discovery; they have different kinds of narrators,
tonalities, ways of presenting material, even different kinds of
foregrounded sentence patterns. The continuity and liveliness that
Naipaul desires in his writing comes only after the descent of the
muse is followed by hard work. Certain conscious formal struc-

tures recur, such as the division of a story or novel into two equal halves, the importance of the centre of the book, the choice between prologues and beginning in the middle of the action, the use of epilogues; but writing not blessed by the muse must be rejected, abandoned, put aside for another time or discarded.

Vidiadhar Surajprasad Naipaul was born in rural Chaguanas, Trinidad, on 17 August 1932. Although his parents were poor his relatives on his mother's side of the family were wealthy. His father, Seepersad (1906–53), was a journalist and one of the first Asian Indians in Trinidad to write about their community. He published a small book of short stories in 1943 and influenced his son's decision to become a writer. Naipaul's younger brother Shiva (1945–85) also became a writer, as has a nephew, Neil Bissoondath. The father suffered for a period from mental problems which caused him to live by himself. This, and other periods of moving house and being at the mercy of others when living among relatives, resulted in Naipaul by the time he was fourteen creating a mask of superior aloofness and left him with a lasting preference for order, style, achievement and solitude. He has questioned how anyone can bring children into this cruel world. His mother's side of the family, the Capildeos, were important among the Orthodox Hindus and include leading Indian Trinidadian politicians. Naipaul's father was modernizing and critical; he at times received death threats from within the family and once was forced into publicly performing an ancient Indian sacrificial ritual. V. S. Naipaul is a rationalist, secular, a strong believer in Western individualism and scepticism, although emotionally attracted towards Indian fatalism, passivity and philosophical notions of the world as illusion. Both world views are together, competing in his writings.

He hated the narrow, circumscribed, brutal life which surrounded him in colonial Trinidad with its limited possibilities, small range of professions, notorious political corruption and racial and religious conflicts. Traditional Indian culture was decaying, its rituals incongruous in Trinidad, and bound for extinction. The Indians among whom he was raised lived in a social world of their own, uninvolved with the other races. The Trinidadians of African descent appeared to have no traditional culture of their own and modelled themselves on the English; their centuries of humiliation resulting in resentment, a brotherhood of skin colour, and fantasies of deliverance. The local whites had produced nothing of lasting value, were drunkards, uneducated, and privileged. They had the best jobs. There was, however, a bond between the descendants of former slaves and slave-owners from which the Indians were excluded and which resulted in the blacks replacing the whites as the dominant group as Trinidad moved towards self-government. Naipaul wanted to escape and had his own fantasies of being one of the early Aryan horsemen who conquered India and created its great Sanskritic culture.

During Naipaul's youth opportunities for education beyond primary schooling were scarce in Trinidad. The only good secondary schools were in Port of Spain; the secondary schools were expensive and there were only a few scholarships available through a national competitive examination. There was no local university until 1970; there were four scholarships to English universities that could be gained through a national examination. After attending primary schools in Chaguanas and Port of Spain, Naipaul won a scholarship to Queen's Royal College in Port of Spain, where he studied French and Spanish and played cricket; he went to Oxford University in 1950 on a Trinidadian government scholarship and received a BA Honours in English in 1953. While at university he suffered a period of mental illness, similar to his father's fear of annihilation, and he remains prone to depression. Soon afterwards he became, until 1956, a freelance writer with the BBC in London. Although he left Trinidad too young and was of the wrong ethnicity to have participated in the black-led cultural developments of the 1950s that accompanied plans for a West Indian Federation, he edited the influential 'Caribbean Voices' which broadcast the new West Indian writing to the region.[3] He married an Englishwoman, Patricia Ann Hale, and the next year, 1956, returned briefly to Trinidad, found it stifling and in the midst of racial and political conflict; his career as a writer was in London.

His first novel, *The Mystic Masseur* (1957), an amusing study of the rise of a West Indian politician from humble beginnings in a rural Hindu community, won the John Llewelyn Rhys Memorial Prize. *The Suffrage of Elvira* (1958) is a comic novel concerning the buying of votes in an isolated, predominantly Hindu community during the second election by universal adult suffrage in Trinidad. *Miguel Street* (1959), a volume of linked short stories which won the Somerset Maugham Award, was actually the first book he had written, although the third to be published. Between 1957 and 1961 he regularly reviewed books for the *New Statesman* in London while writing *A House for Mr Biswas* (1961), his first major novel, an imaginative reconstruction of the Indian experience, his father's life and his own youth in Trinidad. A travel scholarship from the government of Trinidad allowed him to tour the West Indies, at a time when Indian–black tensions were running high, and resulted in *The Middle Passage* (1962), the first of his travel books.

Afterwards he explored the land of his origins, thinking he might live in India. The story of his disillusionment and recognition that he was now a homeless product of colonialism and the new world is told in *An Area of Darkness* (1964). While in India he wrote *Mr Stone and the Knights Companion* (1963), his first novel with an English setting. This began the second phase of his work. Besides not having Trinidadian subject matter the manner is more serious, less openly humorous, more clearly philosophical in its themes. It was awarded the Hawthornden Prize. His feelings of exile, homelessness and disaffection with England, Trinidad and the solitary life of the writer, along with an awareness that he was becoming a voice of the post-colonial world and its discontents, found expression in his second major novel, *The Mimic Men* (1967), which gained the W. H. Smith Prize. *A Flag on the Island* (1967) consists of previously uncollected short stories he wrote at various times, along with a longer satirical story about the cultural and political changes in Trinidad since the 1940s, especially the new nationalism and black racial assertion which he felt to be fabricated by the politicians and influenced by the United States. Its analogies between literary and political mimicry are similar to those found in the novel. The story was originally written for a film, for which the West Indian poet and dramatist Derek Walcott was to do the script, but Naipaul withdrew from the project after disagreement with its sponsors. Between September 1966 and November 1968 he wrote *The Loss of El Dorado* (1969, revised edition 1973), which examines the early history of Trinidad, situating it within such wider events as the European search for gold, and the American, French, Haitian and South American revolutions. Feeling he had made a contribution to Trinidadian national self-awareness and that he could now come to terms with and settle in Trinidad, he sold his London house and returned in time for the 1970 Black Power demonstrations and attempted revolution. He wandered from country to country until his money ran low; he then returned to England where during the next decade he settled.

Although the third period of his writing reveals a sense of despair as he examines the ambiguities of freedom, it includes some of his best work. England became his home from which he travelled to learn and write about other parts of the world. *In a Free State* (1971), which won the Booker Prize, breaks the boundaries between genres, mixing autobiography and fiction. It consists of short stories, a novella and two excerpts from a travel diary, linked by a concern with the problems of freedom for the individual and the decolonized world. *The Overcrowded Barracoon* (1972) is a collection of articles, several of which offer a disillusioning analysis of recurring problems of the small former colonies. The novel *Guerrillas* (1975) has as its background the black power demonstrations, in 1970, and the less well known 1973 guerrilla movement in Trinidad. It explores the social and cultural forces that created such movements, including mimicry of new cultural fashions, and led to the founding of a commune in Trinidad by 'Michael X' who killed some of his followers. Naipaul's investigation of the commune and the murder was originally written for a newspaper and was later republished in '*The Return of Eva Perón' with the 'Killings in Trinidad*' (1980) along with articles discussing Joseph Conrad and 'A New King for the Congo: Mobutu and the Nihilism of Africa'. The reading and travel that went into the later two essays also bore fruit in a major novel, *A Bend in the River* (1979) and a limited edition of *A Congo Diary* (1980).

After his first trip to India Naipaul had to re-examine himself and his career as a writer. He had run through his memories of his time in Trinidad and had outgrown the Evelyn-Waughish comedies of his first novels. Not having been raised in England, not being a white Englishman, he could not write novels about the British class system. Faced by the problem of what to write, he began an analysis of such problems as the conflict between freedom and security in his own life and in the decolonized world. His need for rationality, achievement and order in an otherwise violent, chaotic, purposeless world contributed to his acceptance, in *India: A Wounded Civilization* (1977), of the need for Mrs Gandhi's government to impose a State of Emergency. The discovery of the essential illogicality at the heart of most recent nationalist movements, of wanting the material benefits of modernization while rejecting the civilization and thought that have made such production possible, animates much of his writing of this period including *Among the Believers: An Islamic Journey* (1980). According to Naipaul there is now a Universal Civilization, as represented by

Europe, the United States and Japan, which offers the kind of tolerant society and comforts most people of the world want.[4] To aspire to such freedom and goods while wanting the imagined securities of the past can only result in irrational rage and fantasies. The world has always consisted of change; it is necessary for people and cultures to adapt. This must, however, be done creatively, making use of local resources, and with planning and hard work rather than by mimicry of the former colonial powers.

A new phase of Naipaul's work begins with *Finding the Centre* (1984) which consists of a travel article about the Ivory Coast and 'Prologue to an Autobiography'. The focus has shifted from discussion of the problems of freedom and irritation with irrationality to a celebration of the various people and places Naipaul discovers through travel and writing; he now wants his readers to understand how he works, what goes into his writing. His own past, and his struggle to be a writer, are now less a time of raw anguish than memories recollected in tranquillity. His successful struggle to be a writer and the creation of a world of his own, through travel, settling in a house in England and the transformation of his own experience into literature are celebrated in *The Enigma of Arrival* (1987), a complex, densely written novel which explores the boundaries between autobiography and fiction. Two travel books followed; *A Turn in the South* (1989) sympathetically regards the American South as a place of cultural continuities and religious faith which has unexpected similarities to Trinidadian history. *India: A Million Mutinies* (1990) re-examines his earlier dismissal of Mahatma Gandhi's nationalism and finds the current fragmentation of Indian society a sign of renewal; formerly marginalized, impoverished, passive communities are now creating modern, purposeful lives.

Although Naipaul is a rationalist he has a Brahmin's devotion to study, scholarship, philosophical thought, vocation; there is a Brahminian consciousness of cleanliness, purity, food, and the various duties expected of a well-regulated life. While criticizing Brahmin ritualism and caste discriminations he reveals an interest in and nostalgia for its rituals, and he is aware of caste. His books are of this world, but his characters and autobiographical passages reveal an attraction towards retreat into the spiritual life. Naipaul satirizes Indian notions of fate, but his novels are usually structured around such Indian notions as the four stages of an ordered life – student, marriage and houseowner, retreat into study as a

preparation for total withdrawal from worldliness. There is a continuing conflict in his writings between the chaotic freedom of the
world and the fulfilment of Brahmin ideals. The novels tend to
have a double structure in which events are both seen from a
Western perspective – causality, individual will – and allude to a
Hindu explanation in which the world of desire and things is an
illusion consisting of cycles of creation and destruction. The European perspective dominates, but the Indian world view contests it
and has its attractions.

Naipaul is conscious of himself as an Indian and of his heritage.
He is well read in Indian history and literature. His seemingly
detached understatement (a characteristic found in such Indian
writers as R. K. Narayan and A. K. Ramanujan) can be misleading;
there is concern. The coolness covers anger at injustice, irresponsibility and irrationality. His criticisms of India are those of a
nationalist who feels humiliated by the passivity, factionalism and
traditionalism which allowed foreign conquests of India and which
contributed to the decay of the great Indian civilizations of the
past. *India: A Million Mutinies* reveals a dislike for the Islamic
conquerors of India who for many centuries cruelly and brutally
killed those who opposed them. Naipaul regards the unification of
India under the British during the second half of the nineteenth
century as the beginning of a national revival which led India into
the modern world with a knowledge of itself and its history and
which gave it the concepts that led to independence and growth.

He has often implied that his perspective is not that of a secure
white European liberal preoccupied by historical guilt. Although
slavery and imperialism were terrible crimes, they were not uniquely
European. Africa, India and Islam practised forms of slavery and
continue to do so. Indians have often been the victims of Africans
and Islam. His novels, such as *Guerrillas* and *In a Free State*, reveal a
dislike of white liberals interfering in, and romanticizing, other
societies, about which they know little and from which they can
safely flee the consequences of their interference. Family life in
Trinidad revealed to Naipaul that the world is cruel, competitive,
antagonistic, a war for advantage. Imperialism can even be desir-
able if it brings order, peace, security and knowledge and raises
people to a larger, more tolerant view of the world beyond their
petty local conflicts and limited vision.

Naipaul's perspective has been shaped by the humiliations of his
youth; it is also influenced by his consciousness of being Indian

and the humiliations India has suffered. Its weakness led to its people being shipped around the world as indentured labour, the abandonment of the Indians in black-dominated Trinidad and Guyana, the expulsions of Indians from Africa.[5] Although he avoids the useless, self-defeating, self-wounding rhetoric of protest and resentment, his writings note the humiliation of Indians whether during the Islamic conquests, the British destruction of the former Indian economy, the fear felt by Trinidadian Indians towards Negro policemen or the confiscation of Indian businesses in postcolonial Africa. He writes often about the condition of India and the Indian diaspora, of which he is part. He sees his travels as analogous to those of the diaspora as displaced Indians journey through the modern world attempting to create a home elsewhere and as they revise their history to explain their own predicament.

Brought in the mid-nineteenth century to the West Indies, especially Guyana and Trinidad, to replace the freed black slaves, the Indians were indentured labourers on contracts with few rights. The British later refused to pay for their return. In Trinidad the Indians reformed their societies, even restoring caste distinctions, and purchased land for farming, but they remained isolated from the dominant white and black communities, without education in English and without legal consideration. Hindu marriages, for example, were for many decades unrecognized by law. During Naipaul's childhood impoverished homeless Indians who spoke only Hindi were still expecting to return some day to Mother India.

When talk of independence came to Trinidad the Hindu Indians felt insecure, fearing being left by the British under the dominance of the brown and black communities which had organized themselves politically and which, concentrated in the cities and having gained access to English language education, staffed the police and civil service and influenced the government. The British Labour Party wanted decolonization and favoured such black intellectuals as Eric Williams, who had studied in England. But for a Trinidadian Indian the rhetoric of decolonization was filled with black nationalism, pan-Africanism, Judaeo-Christian notions of black racial deliverance and Marxist models of single party states. In such a situation the Hindu Indian was the outsider, the marginal, the opposition to those who felt destined to inherit the apparatus of the state at independence.

Eric Williams, who led Trinidad to self-government and independence, was a brilliant, ruthless politician who demanded discipline and who treated violently those whom he considered enemies; opposition political leaders were ruined and forced into exile. Those within the ruling party who opposed its corruption and waste were destroyed. Williams built his party around a rhetoric of black nationalism while cooperating with the local white business community. He found a place for the Indian Moslems but treated Hindu Indians as enemies and regarded their opposition to national independence as treason.[6] Elections were characterized by violence and by Indian claims that the results were rigged. Agriculture, the area of the economy dominated by Indians, was neglected. It was only after Williams' death that Indians shared in the government; even now tension can run high between blacks and Indians in Trinidad.

In nearby Guyana during the 1950s the nationalist movement split into rival Indian and black parties; the Indian socialists who won the elections were twice deposed, first by the British and later with American help. There have been bloody inter-racial riots and the country has been ruled by a tyrannical black nationalist government which led it to economic ruin and refused to hold fair elections. Naipaul's view of decolonization has been influenced by such events and he has taken such knowledge with him on his travels where it has been confirmed by his observations about the situation of minorities in Africa and other parts of the third world.

Although Naipaul is a realist, and his writings are filled with factual details and based on observations about the actual world, such a description does not do justice to him or to his work. As a writer he has always been conscious of literary models and conventions which he uses, parodies and revises. Often his models are a subtext providing contrasts to his own subject matter and the societies he portrays. There is a continuous and evolving struggle to find the right shape for his material and vision. This ranges from learning how to write about the East Indian community in Trinidad as its traditions decayed and it entered the national community, to learning how to write about his own attempts to understand himself. His fiction became more psychological, complex, distanced in tone, drier, less amusing, as he attempted to understand the world and his characters. As he became conscious of the private sources of his vision, including his reading, and willing to reveal them, his writing mixed autobiography with the fictional and the observed world. As literary genres blur together the writing becomes more self-referential and filled with literary allusions and echoes. There are more gaps permitted, less causality visible in the narrative. Even his travel writing evolved: recent books appear more filled with the voices of others. As he allows the material to express itself, as he leaves room for contrasting opinions, his conclusions come as a surprise.

His evolving complexity as a writer is especially seen in his treatment of sex and women. The early fiction is critical of the brutality with which West Indian men treat women, while seeing sexual desire as a temptation which interferes with a person's rational decisions. Romantic love in his novels is often self-destructive. In the later novels he shows how male sexual insecurity leads to sadism and hatred of women while women themselves are often masochistically attracted towards brutality. Because Naipaul has scenes of sexual violence in his fiction he sometimes has been regarded as anti-women.

When Naipaul was a student in Trinidad and even when he began publishing in England there was little Trinidadian literature. Except for Claude McKay (1889–1948) and Jean Rhys (1894–1979), exiles many decades earlier from Jamaica and Dominica, and a few sporadic minor early figures, West Indian literature of serious interest only began to develop in the 1940s and 50s with such novels as Edgar Mittelholzer's *Corentyne Thunder* (1941), Samuel Selvon's *A Brighter Sun* (1952), George Lamming's *In the Castle of My Skin* (1954), John Hearne's *Voices under the Window* (1955) and Naipaul's own *The Mystic Masseur* (1957).[7] Naipaul was part of the movement during the 1950s towards a distinctly West Indian literature; he was involved in the 'Caribbean Voices' programme; he used local subject matter and dialect; in London he performed the part of Hounakin in a West Indian production of Derek Walcott's play *The Sea at Dauphin*. His analysis of the problems of colonial Trinidad is similar to that of other West Indian writers of the time. As it lacked any local literary market, any local publishers interested in local writing, and any local readership, the writers were expatriates living and publishing in London.

There was, however, a small body of Trinidadian literature from the 1930s onwards written by a group that was first associated with two short-lived magazines, *Trinidad* and *The Beacon* (1931–3). Albert Gomes, Alfred Mendes and C. L. R. James were nationalists and progressive politicians who wrote fiction during the 1930s about working-class life in the 'barracks', especially the lives of blacks.

Naipaul's father, Seepersad, was in contact with a related literary circle; in 1947 this group published an anthology, mostly of poetry, that included Seepersad's 'They Named him Mohun', which Naipaul used as the basis of the opening section of *A House for Mr Biswas*.[8] It was Seepersad Naipaul's own self-published short stories in *Gurudeva and other Indian Tales* (1943, which his son revised for republication in 1976 as *The Adventures of Gurudeva and Other Stories*) which began Indian writing about their community in Trinidad and which showed Naipaul how he could write about the world he had known as a child.

Seepersad avoided the West Indian middle-class literary tradition of political and racial protest, of sentimentality and anger, with its contrasts between white and black, rich and poor, European and Creole. Instead he wrote about the rural Indian community from within; he wrote about it objectively and with a touch of satire, aware that its traditions were ossifying and becoming sterile as a result of distance from their land of origins. This was the starting point for Naipaul's own writing, to which he brought a superior education and familiarity with the classics of literature, a heightened sense of structure, a greater dedication to the art of writing, the advantages of exile, distance and opportunities to publish in England. Naipaul's early fiction brought to West Indian writing the social awareness and comedy characteristic of British fiction, the sense of form and economy found in the early fiction of James Joyce, a Proustian awareness of change, time and memory. He brought a new depth and seriousness to West Indian fiction while bringing it up to date. While Samuel Selvon (b. 1923), another Trinidadian Indian novelist who began publishing before Naipaul, has a similar sense of humour, he is a less accomplished writer, somewhat limited to the problems and comedy of Indian, black and white relationships. Naipaul brought the West Indian novel into the mainstream of contemporary English language fiction at a time that Derek Walcott was establishing West Indian poetry and drama as being worth international attention. They were part of a generation of writers, including Wole Soyinka and Chinua Achebe in Nigeria, whose decolonization of English literature parallels the political changes of our time.

The literary market for West Indian writers was also changing. Writing about his father's lack of opportunities Naipaul has said:

> A reading to a small group, publication in a magazine soon lost to view: writing in Trinidad was an amateur activity, and this

was all the encouragement a writer could expect. There were no magazines that paid; there were no established magazines . . . My father was a purely local writer, and writers like that ran the risk of ridicule.

Attitudes began to change when Derek Walcott of St Lucia gained attention by publishing locally his first volume of poems in 1949 – it was soon republished in Barbados – and when Edgar Mittelholzer's novel about Trinidad, *A Morning at the Office*, was published in England. 'And then there at least appeared a market.' The BBC 'Caribbean Voices' took local writing seriously, had standards and paid well enough 'to spread a new idea of the value of writing'.[9] Naipaul was part of this change both as an editor for 'Caribbean Voices' and through his own success as a writer.

Naipaul's philosophy of life might be called 'existential'. Although later influenced by his reading of Albert Camus and Jean-Paul Sartre, he appears to have come to such views through his own observation and experience of the world. People must create themselves, leave their mark on history, or they are annihilated. An appearance of effortless superiority and style is preferred, but achievement requires hard work, ambition, will, cunning, even brutality. Losers shout resentment and cry victimization instead of thinking clearly about their situation and helping themselves. There is also in Naipaul a nostalgia for 'home', for continuity and community, for being settled, for shared values. Ideally the individual will towards self-creation should find expression within a community that has a sense of its past, an idea of itself and a will towards leaving its mark on history. Without such a community, individuals struggle against their environment, a struggle that is painful and likely to be limiting. But such ideal communities are seldom found; rather the historian or writer imagines such an ideal order out of the struggles for power and the achievements in the past. Yet such an idea of order and purpose is needed by individuals and society. Naipaul is sceptical of the possibility of many small nations becoming truly independent; he regards the hasty grouping of diverse peoples into new nations as likely to lead to civil war and tyranny. Such nations seldom have an idea of themselves based upon their actual circumstances.

In a recent book about post-colonial theory Naipaul is said to have 'one of the clearest visions of the nexus of power operating in the imperial-colonial world' but 'he is paradoxically drawn to that centre even though he sees it constructing the "periphery" as an area of nothingness. Yet he is simultaneously able to see that the "reality", "the truth", and "order" of the centre is also an illusion.' This concisely expresses several of Naipaul's themes, and shows why he has one of the most analytical perspectives on the post-colonial world. But it leaves out such matters which have gone into Naipaul's writings as the effect upon him of his youth in Trinidad, discrimination against Indians in many parts of the 'third world', the struggle to earn a living as a writer, his vision of life being brief, insecure, without purpose, a jungle of warring groups, unless it is given purpose through achievement, continuity, an ideal of order backed by real power. It also leaves out the attraction of giving up the struggle, accepting nothingness, withdrawing into inactivity, Indian fatalism. While the critics claim that 'There is no centre of reality just as there is no pre-given unmediated reality',[10] there is a great difference between a philosophical argument and lived reality. Life in contemporary Australia, New Zealand or Canada may not be significantly different from that in England or the United States, but that was not true in the past and is still not true of Zaire or even Trinidad. Naipaul is aware of such problems and has expressed them in his writings. For psychological and practical reasons, as well as from his experience of the world, he desires order, freedom and achievement. Writing creates the narrative order that the world lacks; through it we can understand and celebrate ourselves.

2

Miguel Street, The Mystic Masseur and The Suffrage of Elvira

While Naipaul's first three books of fiction are extraordinarily popular because of their comedy, implicit are such themes as the way impoverished, hopeless lives and the chaotic mixing of cultures result in fantasy, brutality, violence and corruption. The three books are also social history showing the start of protest politics during the late 1930s and how Trinidad began to change during and after the Second World War. The infusion of American money and the beginnings of local self-government created new possibilities where few existed before; but such social change is treated amusingly, without the more analytical perspective found in later novels.

The origins of *Miguel Street* (1959), a volume of linked short stories, can be found in 'Prologue to an Autobiography' (1982) where Naipaul recalls thirty years earlier, in a room of the BBC in London, writing the first sentence of 'Bogart' from his memories of Trinidad. It was one of those gifts from the muse that writers need to get started:

> The first sentence was true. The second was invention. But together – to me, the writer – they had done something extraordinary. Though they had left out everything – the setting, the historical time, the racial and social complexities of the people concerned – they had suggested it all; they had created the world of the street. And together, as sentences, words, they had set up a rhythm, a speed, which dictated all that was to follow. (*Finding the Centre*, p. 19)

17

V. S. Naipaul

The antiphonal refrain 'What's happening there, Bogart?', 'What's happening there, Hat?' brought to the surface memories of people and the life he had known in Port of Spain and soon a small world, full of its own life and ways, having its own unique manners and morals, was sketched in. Naipaul's subject was an impoverished area of Port of Spain with its cultural diversity, fantasies, chaotic and changing standards, its fashions and imitation of style, its mistaken notions of masculinity and mistreatment of women, its self-defeating excuses, its limitations and the improbability of achievement from those living in such an environment.

The tales reflect a time when Naipaul's family had moved from the enclosed Indian world of the countryside to the more ethnically varied Port of Spain. Miguel Street is a racially mixed community predominantly black, brown and Indian but with some Spanish, Portuguese and 'whites'. Although to the boy who narrates the stories the men lounging on the streets represent community standards, the people seem in transit and houses rapidly change owners. Miguel Street is not exactly a slum as its inhabitants look down on those areas where the people are dirtier, poorer or rougher. Style is important to the men as it is a way of asserting visibility in an impoverished colonial society which offers few opportunities for riches, fame or achievement. Style may be a matter of imitating a current movie star like Bogart, noticeable eccentric behaviour, mystification about the past, or an apparently careless disregard for social conventions (Laura has eight children by seven fathers). Status may be gained by having, like Eddoes, a night job as a garbageman, allowing freedom from work during the day and the display of a uniform along with the pickings of the trash of the wealthy in other parts of Port of Spain. Style is the underdog's way of being unique, a way to assert identity, a mask for failure.

Many of the stories evolve from the boy's admiration of the pretences of those around him to a revelation of failure. B. Wordsworth claims to be writing a great poem and tells of a tragic love affair, but he is an unemployed calypso singer who has never written poetry; his romantic love story is a lie. Popo busies himself with carpentry, supposedly making some ideal 'Thing Without a Name', but he makes nothing; the furnishings of his house are found to be stolen. In many of the stories the entrance or exit of a woman from a man's life leads to some major change in behaviour and the central character is arrested by the police. In Miguel Street nothing is made, no business succeeds, no art work is finished, no love or marriage lasts.

Miguel Street differs from Steinbeck's *Cannery Row* and Joyce's *Dubliners* in its social comedy and seeming lightness of tone, the impression of business and activity. Bogart may be 'the most bored man I know' (p. 9) and the boy when he grows up and leaves school may turn to drinking and whoring because 'What else anybody can do here except drink?' (p. 167) but the narration does not romanticize, sentimentalize, or protest; rather there is a Trinidadian world of the carnivalesque in the public displays of imitated and assumed character. Everyone appears to be play-acting in public, creating small dramas. In Miguel Street there is a tolerance, even an appreciation, of eccentric self-display.

Incongruity between pretence and reality is characteristic of Miguel Street. Gestures, words and ideas do not have the same meaning in an impoverished colonial society as elsewhere. What appears self-expressive turns out to be a lie, masks for failure, and is the result of Trinidad being a colonial backwater, a place without the means to enable a better life. Even leaving is difficult. There is worse poverty elsewhere in the West Indies as is shown by the Grenadians coming to Trinidad. Qualifications for better jobs can only be gained by taking British examinations. In a colony which then had no university and few secondary schools, further education means going abroad, and that requires money or one of the few government scholarships. It also means a break with the past and facing an alien, more competitive world without the support of family, friends and excuses. When the narrator does leave at the conclusion he is 'looking only at my shadow before me, a dancing dwarf on the tarmac' (p. 172).

'Man-man', an often anthologized story from *Miguel Street*, shows that Naipaul had already devised the methods and structures he would often use in his books. While detailed criticism is out of fashion at present, an analysis will be useful towards understanding what is consistent and what changes as his fiction evolves. Like many of Naipaul's narratives, 'Man-man' is based on fact; there was a well known person like him in Port of Spain.[11] The selectivity of presentation means that there is a subtext of implied explanations to be inferred; the larger significances are understated. He binds together the narrative and the prose by repetition of sounds, words, phrases, sentence patterns, images, parallel and analogous events. What seems simple and easy, almost natural story telling, will be found to be highly crafted towards continuity, movement and the symbolic. While the prose is economical, straightforward, rapid in movement and clear in its presentation, its sound patterns are richly textured, creating a sense of organic flow. There are, for instance, the 'm' sounds in the first paragraph: Miguel, Man-man, mad, him, am, mad, many, much, madder, Man-man. The second paragraph picks up the 'm's: 'He didn't look mad. He was a man of medium height' (p. 38). The continuity and movement are built from repetitions and variations. The method of organization of sound and connectives is a model for the story and the book, which move rapidly while being tightly woven and organized.

'Man-man' is organized by two contrasting halves. In the first half there are a number of seemingly discontinuous episodes, which reveal character, circumstances, desires and context, but which suggest a lack of direction, an aimless shuffling around, and which end in a failure requiring a new start. The second half shows the character driven by some new prospect, rises in excitement, develops and expands the possibilities, has continuity, but instead of a climax there is a burst bubble, a rapid descent. Within this scheme there are other clearly articulated sections, especially in the first half; the second half is more continuous as the story gathers together its themes for what at first appears a new start.

After the introduction (I.1) to character and theme – 'Everyone in Miguel Street said that Man-man was mad' (p. 38) – there is a small character sketch ('He was a man of medium height, thin') and the raising of the question of whether Man-man is really so different from 'everybody' on Miguel Street ('I can think of many people much madder than Man-man ever was'). The use of the past tense creates a double perspective, the narrator as a child when he saw the events he is narrating and the mature speaker with his sense of judgement and distance. From the very first sentence a contrast is created between the community, 'Everybody', and the lonely, eccentric Man-man. As the story develops we see that his fantasy life is not unlike that of the rest of the community. Each section is clearly articulated with a conclusion, transitional sentence or introduction: 'But he did have some curious habits.' I.2 concerns Man-man's eccentric political life: 'He went up for every election.' The absurdity of his campaign parodies politics in Trinidad at that time, when candidates were independent personalities without a party. 'They just had the word "Vote" and below that, Man-man's picture.' Yet at every election two others always vote for Man-man.

Hat provides another perspective and focus besides that of the narrator, the community and Man-man. Hat is the voice of adult sanity and experience: 'they must be funny sort of jokers if they do

the same thing so many times. They must be mad just like he.'
Hat's speech with its West Indian grammar contrasts to the stand-
ard English of the narrator and creates a sense of the culture and
society in which the story takes place. The lack of grammatical
coordination implies a society with different, fractured norms and
values. Section I.3 begins 'Man-man never worked'; he passes the
time scrolling a single word on the sidewalk. The parallel is to the
boy's education at school. The status symbols and educational
system in colonial Trinidad are inappropriate to the reality. Its
Britishness is mimicry: 'If you shut your eyes while he spoke, you
would believe an Englishman – a good-class Englishman who wasn't
particular about grammar – was talking to you' (p. 39). Man-man
is another of Naipaul's characters who is a failed writer or artist.

In Man-man's madness there is cunning, aggressiveness and a
kind of rationality. After he barks like a dog in a café and is ejected
(I.4) he manages to enter the café after it has closed and leaves
'little blobs of excrement' (p. 40) on every stool and table and
at regular intervals along the counter. People laugh at the owner
of the café rather than feeling sympathy or outrage. Humiliation
of others is admirable by local values. Hat says 'These people
are really bad-mind'. The character-sketch of the dog, I.5, is an
amusing parallel to the previous description of Man-man, even
echoing some of the same words ('curious', 'never'), and suggests
a similar sense of isolation: 'It never made friends with any other
dog'; but there is affection between Man-man and his dog. 'They
were made for each other.' Man-man has trained his dog to
defecate on command (I.6), and it soils clothes left by others
to bleach overnight; people then give the clothes to Man-man who
sells them. Man-man becomes a local hero, similar to the con-men,
the tricksters, who in *The Middle Passage* Trinidadians are said to
admire: 'all the people who had suffered from Man-man's dog
were anxious to get other people to suffer the same thing' (p. 41).

The story until now illustrates what in *The Middle Passage* Naipaul
describes as a picaroon society with its lack of responsibility, its
animosity, aggression, taste for corruption, lack of respect for the
person, lack of rigid social conventions, its natural anarchy, cynicism and eccentricity (pp. 80–3). The story has evolved from a
character sketch to an indirect sketch of a community and its
unusual values. While Man-man is alone the story feels populated
by lots of 'Everybody' and how they respond to what he does.

The first half of 'Man-man' evolves from snippets to longer
episodes. The second half, which is more unified, has continuity

and concerns Man-man's religious conversion and his attempted self-crucifixion. The second half begins with a clear transition when Man-man turns 'good' (which will be found to be, like 'curious' or 'men of mystery', ironic; it directs attention to further implications beyond Man-man's conversion). The death of the dog ('it gave, Hat said, one short squeak') foreshadows the end of the story, while providing an explanation of Man-man's change in behaviour, caused by the need to find some new source of income, a new business to replace selling dog-soiled clothes. Man-man's conversion to become a preacher, like much of Naipaul's humour, depends on incongruity: 'he said he had seen God after having a bath' (p. 41). After the character sketch ('He began talking to himself, clasping his hands'), Naipaul immediately expands the relevance of the story from Miguel Street to all of Trinidad, by alluding to its factual basis (a spiritualism masseur was an important local politician and member of the legislature). Section II.1 concludes amusingly, 'I suppose it was natural that since God was in the area Man-man should see Him' (p. 41). Man-man (II.2) preaches against political independence, does well financially in his collections and begs for food, claiming he is following the ways of Jesus (II.3).

Having found a successful career that does not require a trained dog, Man-man becomes carried away and announces he is the 'new Messiah' who is going to 'crucify hisself' (p. 43). He writes notices saying that he will 'tie hisself to a cross and let people stone him' (p. 43). Amusement with local streetcorner preachers is blended with satire on how readily Trinidadians take to such movements. Man-man is a con-man, fantasist, half-mad and, like the other characters in the stories, driven by an inner need to find a social role through creating an imposing identity to compensate for the limitations of his life. There is a frightening if amusing contrast between the facts and the seriousness with which the community regards Man-man's imitation of Christ (II.4). When Hat tells of a rumour that the cross is made of matchwood and is light, Edward snaps, 'That matter? Is the heart and the spirit that matter' (p. 43). A truck takes the cross, instead of Man-man carrying it (II.5), and as soon as people begin throwing large stones at Man-man on his cross he looks 'hurt and surprised' (p. 44), demands to be untied and threatens to 'go settle with that son of a bitch who pelt a stone at me'. But the crowd continues to throw stones while he shouts 'I finish with this arseness, you hear'. Man-man is for once normal, while it is the crowd that is mad; the community has become violent. Only after his fantasy life collapses is Man-man removed from the community, to an insane asylum. The last words of the story, 'Then for good', echo the 'to turn good' with which the second half begins.

'Man-man' is similar to the stories in the first half of *Miguel Street* in its two-part structure, its reversal of tonality and the expansion of themes in its second half, the role of someone who is depended upon (wife, dog), in the transformation of the character's behaviour, of the way the character becomes carried away by a fantasy which he or she is unable to keep up when faced by an increase in the pressures of reality, the centrality of acting as opposed to a real character, and this way the story rapidly ends in an anti-climax, humiliation, defeat and the coming of the police.

The madness of Man-man's preaching, which becomes part of his crucifixion fantasy, is frightening and related to the otherwise extraneous political topics – the two people who vote for Man-man year after year, the talk of political independence. Man-man became a leader of the crowd, an example of West Indian politics rooted in personalities and the desire for deliverance and salvation, the combination of the political and the religious that has so often been characteristic of political leadership in the New World and which was noticeable in Eric Williams and other black nationalist leaders during the late colonial and early independence periods. Oxaal says both lower and middle-class Negroes saw Williams as 'a Messiah come to lead the black children into the Promised Land'.[12] 'Man-man' is more than an amusing tale of eccentricity. It shows how distress and lack of accepted social standards rapidly become fantasy and violence, and produce leaders without any clear programme but who provide public drama. The story looks forward to Naipaul's study of black power movements, and especially the events in Trinidad in 1970 and 1973, in *Guerrillas*. Man-man's ability to be carried away by a self-dramatizing fantasy might be said to be similar to the pointlessness of Fisheye's hijacking of a police jeep and announcement that it is the beginning of a people's revolution in another Trinidadian novel, Earl Lovelace's *The Dragon Can't Dance* (1979). Significantly Lovelace's novel begins with:

This is the hill tall above the city where Taffy, a man who say he is Christ, put himself up on a cross one burning midday and say to his followers: 'Crucify me! Let me die for my people. Stone me with stones as you stone Jesus, I will love you still.' And when they start to stone him in truth he get vex and start to cuss: 'Get me down! Get me down!' he say.[13]

The structure of *Miguel Street* as a book is similar to that of 'Manman'. The various stories are linked subsections of a larger story concerning the narrator and his relationship to Hat, which comes to a conclusion in the next-to-last story of the volume and which is followed by the narrator's disillusionment and departure for England. The first half of the book has two sections. 'Bogart' to 'The Coward' are tales of failure which follow a pattern of amusing fantasy followed by deflation. Each central character is a mockery of some ideal: Popo is a philosopher, Morgan is a comedian. There is often a clear break, loss of wife, temporary disappearance or loss of direction by the main character, then a change as the story becomes more serious, reality is found to be more dangerous and violent than it first appeared, often the police come and the fantasy collapses and the character is defeated or found to be a fake. As the volume proceeds the stories become more complex, as humiliations are shown to be the basis of the eccentricities which produce local heroes, heroes who are fraudulent and dangerous. Big Foot compensates for childhood humiliations by acting like a dangerous bully; but he does win his boxing matches until he is defeated by a supposed RAF champion and begins crying in the boxing ring. In a extra twist we learn that the champion was a fake, a complete unknown. After these early stories ending in defeat are two transitional tales, 'The Pyrotechnicist' and 'Titus Hoyt, I.A.', in which the central character seemingly overcomes a personal history of failure to triumph, but the triumph itself is pathetic. Morgan finally gets recognition as a maker of fireworks when he burns down his house and runs away. While this is Naipaul the ironist, it shows the personal and social consequences of distress.

The early stories show a world of men without purpose. While the men treat their women as inferiors, their world is held together by women; the failure of the men is typified by their relation to, and lack of, women. This is anticipated in Bogart with his humiliation at not being able to have children and his deserting his wives to: 'Be a man, among we men' (p. 14). These men are illustrations of the weakness of the West Indian male, his inability and unwillingness to be responsible for a family and a woman. It is the women who are strong. Morgan tries to act like a patriarch, but wanting the approval of other men he carries on supposedly comic public trials of his children and when this backfires he gets drunk and bellows: 'You people think I am not a man, eh? My father had eight children. I his son. I have ten. I better than all of you put together' (p. 69). Morgan tries to prove his manliness by an affair with Teresa Blake, is caught by his wife and publicly humiliated: 'Mrs Morgan was holding up Morgan by his waist. He was practically naked, and he looked so thin, he was like a boy with an old man's face' (p. 71). In reading these stories and *A House for Mr Biswas* it might be remembered that the duties of a Brahmin include education and having a house and family.

The stories in *Miguel Street* usually take place in public. Naipaul has commented that in the West Indies life is public, unlike in England where life takes place indoors behind shut doors and curtained windows. But the Trinidadian camaraderie of the street is seen as hollow, something the boy outgrows as he learns it is a world of failure, of talk rather than achievement. The Indians, blacks, whites are adrift, aimless, culturally, socially, politically, economically and ethically impoverished, without realizable ideals. Thus the humiliations, eccentricity, play-acting, brutality and failure.

After 'Titus Hoyt' there is a deepening of emotion, the characters become more complex or there is a recognition of tragedy. Laura may be heroic as the archetypical West Indian matriarch, having children by different men, surviving on her wits and what she can get from her men, but when her own unmarried daughter has a child and starts to repeat the cycle of West Indian womanhood she feels it would be better for her daughters to die than to be like herself. Contrasted to the women of Miguel Street is Mrs Hereira who descends from the rich secure white world, leaving her almost perfect husband, for a drunk who violently beats her. A story concerning the relationship of sexual desire to sadism, masochism and love, it also anticipates Naipaul's later novels, such as *Guerrillas*, where well-off whites, bored with their security, look for emotional excitement by playing at being unconventional and idealistic, expecting that when life becomes dangerous they can return to the safe world from which they came. Mrs Hereira is a forerunner of Jane in *Guerrillas* and Yvette in *A Bend in the River*. Romantic love is a luxury of the rich white. The boy's mother, an Indian, says: 'If somebody did marry you off when you was fifteen,

we wouldnta been hearing all this nonsense, you hear. Making all
this damn fuss about your heart and love and all that rubbish' (p.
111). Naipaul's novels differ from most European and American
fiction in portraying romantic love and sexual freedom as destructive, a dereliction of one's real duties. The perspective is Indian
rather than European.

Indian attitudes are often playfully present in the stories. Uncle
Bhakcu, 'The Mechanical Genius', reads the *Ramayana* every day
and succeeds as a pundit, although a West Indian one crawling
under cars trying to be a Western mechanic while 'Hindus waited
for him to attend to their souls' (p. 127). In 'His Chosen Calling'
Eddoes, from a low Hindu caste, is a sweeper and proud of his
inheritance. British social comedy is tinged by Hindu notions of
caste and fate.

Some stories have allusions to or quotations from calypsos. Originally from Trinidad, the calypso is brutal in its comments on topic
events. The difference between calypso and the newer Soca (a
mixture of calypso and black American soul music) is that the
former gives priority to the words and is satiric, the latter to music
and is for dancing. While Naipaul's use of calypso adds to the
colour and realism of his stories it also shows the likely Trinidadian
response in contrast to the innocence of the boy narrator; the
calypso represents the harsh actualities of the society in contrast to
the humanism and sympathy for characters inherent to the conventions of European fiction. Naipaul has often written with approval of the direct honesty of Trinidadian discussion of such
matters as race when he was younger. Like the Calypsonian he
observes and comments without sentimental illusions.

The calypsos are also social history and are used, along with
references to films, cricket matches and well known events to
create a record of Trinidad for a decade from the late 1930s until
after the war. Approximately twelve years pass, the boy narrator is
eight years old at the start, over eighteen at the conclusion. At the
start Trinidad is a colony dependent on England, then the war
brings the Americans with their money, new kinds of social relations, attitudes, jobs; next come elections and talk of independence. There are two frames of reference: history as seen locally,
local history in relationship to the wider world. Such use of an
outside, European historical frame of reference was common to
many works of fiction of the late colonial and early independence
period when writers had both to put local society on the literary

map and to relate its chronology to what foreign readers would know. Later writers would no longer feel that such a broad perspective was necessary. They had become more confident that readers were interested in fiction told from a Trinidadian, Indian or African angle; the former colonies had become less marginal to modern history. When Titus Hoyt takes the unwilling boys to Fort George and tells them that the fort was built in 1803 when the French were planning to invade Trinidad, and 'we was fighting Napoleon', the boys are stunned as: 'We had never realized that anyone considered us so important' (p. 81).

The stories allude to a time when Trinidad was important for its plantations, a former economy which is recalled by the remains of decaying buildings. There is a history here, a possible 'usable past', when Trinidad was a significant place in the Empire and part of world trade and worth fighting over in contrast to the impoverished, neglected Trinidad of the 1930s and 40s in which the outside world seems distant and incomprehensible to Bolo and others.

Miguel Street consists of memories of a lost childhood homeland. Nostalgia is the usual subject matter of the first book of an expatriate colonial writer. Unlike such books as, say, Camara Laye's *L'Enfant noir*, there is in *Miguel Street* little sentimentality for paradise lost, none of the expatriate's usual yearning for the protection of family, tribe, friends, unquestioned customs and obligations. Naipaul may have felt such emotions, and from his comments in 'Prologue to an Autobiography' and *The Enigma of Arrival* there is reason to think that Trinidad remains emotionally 'home' in contrast to the alienation of exile, but the short stories are astringent in their ironies. They are his *Dubliners* and *A Portrait of the Artist as a Young Man*. They show why it was necessary to leave and remain away from home.

The developing perspective of the boy narrator as he grows up shows his understanding that a period of his life has ended, the secure world he knew has fragmented; Hat, his adult mentor (the substitute father figure in the stories), has aged, become crazed for a woman, been jailed and broken. If the narrator does not leave Trinidad he will soon become another failure like those he mistakenly admired. Even the Americans have departed, packed up their base and left, taking with them the money, attitudes and new opportunities which became available during the war years. Under the comedy is criticism of 'home' and its acceptance of its fate and habits of accepting defeat. Bolo, in 'Caution', fails so often at everything he does that when he wins some money on the sweepstake he refuses to believe it, as it would destroy his sense of being a victim, and tears up the ticket and withdraws into himself. It is easier to blame the imperial powers or racial discrimination or Trinidadian corruption than to accept his own past foolishness and failures of character.

Naipaul's concern with the decay of traditional Hindu Trinidad and the incongruities of its existence within a predominantly black, Westernized, national community of various cultures results in irony, comedy, absurdity, when English words and ideals do not apply to what actually happens. Particularly in politics, there is a misfit between liberal notions of representation and decolonization and the realities of society in a late colonial or newly independent state. In *The Mystic Masseur* and *The Suffrage of Elvira* politics are a vehicle for Trinidadian Hindus to become part of a larger national society; but the politics are for personal gain and advancement rather than those of social justice, ethnic dignity and independence. In *The Mystic Masseur* Pundit Ganesh moves easily through various roles and careers as is fitting to someone who is part of, and representative of, a larger cultural change which the Indians share with the other Trinidadians as the island evolves towards independence. But there are the resulting incongruities as an unsuccessful Hindu masseur becomes, through the study of modern psychology, a rich successful medicine man for the black Trinidadians and then a leading national politician who is eventually knighted by the British. Throughout the novel we are made aware of the contrast between the Hindu notion of karma or fate which Ganesh claims to follow and the stubbornness and cunning of his personality. The cultural confusion he represents is echoed in the various ways his tale could be told – as an illustration of fate or as a New World version of the European novel of personal will, ambition and success.

The Mystic Masseur (1957) is Evelyn Waughish in its speed, economy, understated satiric ironies, incongruities, comedy, undeveloped characterization, and unexpected changes in the direction of the plot, contrasts between what is said and done, parody and the ironic placing of characters by a few details of the scene or by habits of speech. The narration is tinged with small as well as larger ironies. As we follow the evolution of Ganesh's life the descriptions, scenes and events are often in contrast to what we understand. At Government Training College for teachers in Port of Spain, Ganesh 'was taught many important subjects and from time to time he practised on little classes from schools near by. He learned to write on a blackboard . . .' (p. 23). Within a few words three topics are quietly ridiculed, the courses taken in colleges of education, blackboard training and the improbability that practising on small select classes will prepare teachers. A few pages later we see the reality of local education: 'If you leave the boys alone, they leave you alone' (p. 25). While the characters in *The Mystic Masseur* are often grotesques, Dickens' caricatures, much of the comedy comes from the economical insertion of ironies ('the stimulating peace and quiet of the country' [p. 31]) or absurdities ('Is his father dead, you know. His only father' [p. 30]).

In spite of the seemingly ironic claim to be a story of 'a hero of the people' (p. 11) and 'the history of our times' (p. 18), *The Mystic Masseur* is both. Those familiar with Trinidadian history should recognize how Naipaul has used local events, characters and such politicians as Uriah Butler, Albert Gomes, Arthur Cipriani and Naipaul's two uncles, Rudranath and Simbhoonath Capildeo, in his novel.[14] A mystic masseur was an independent member of the legislative council; the masseur's practice of getting headlines by walking out, or having to be carried out, from the legislature was Albert Gomes' method; the last stages of Naipaul's masseur's political career (the misjudging of the mood of strikers, the conservative turn, the international conferences) seemingly are based on Cipriani and Gomes. Naipaul's early fiction is based on memories of Trinidadian cultural and political life before he left for England in 1950. He creatively brings together characteristics of various political leaders. Ganesh's rise to political prominence took place at a time, immediately after the Second World War, when the British were rapidly trying to unburden themselves of their colonies, but before real political parties had been formed in the colonies. It was a transitional period of flamboyant personalities rather than party organization and ideologies. These were the first elections to the legislature by universal adult suffrage, in contrast to appointed representatives. It was also a period when Trinidadian politics were notably corrupt and when some of the politicians were intellectuals who had studied in England:

> [Indarsingh's] speeches were long, carefully thought-out things
> – later published by the author in book form with the title

Colonialism: Four Essays – about The Economics of Colonialism, Colonialism in Perspective, The Anatomy of Oppression, The Approach to Freedom. Indarsingh travelled about with his own blackboard and a box of coloured chalks, illustrating his arguments with diagrams. Children liked him. (p. 201)

Indarsingh is a version of a character who will reappear in Naipaul's novels, the Indian who attends a famous British university and returns to Trinidad with superior but inappropriate and ineffectual attitudes. (Several such politicians were family relatives.) British political culture is seen as absurd in Trinidad when at the time, 1946, there was no strong sense of nationhood and a common past, little education, little political discussion, no political ideals or policies. Ganesh is an Indian version of Man-man, the unemployed, apparently untalented, marginal man who finds a career and employment first in religion and then as a leader of the people.

Naipaul's depiction of Trinidadian politics is amusing, but his laughter is defensive. His method is to invert and treat ironically what influences and concerns him. If *The Mystic Masseur* is a parody *bildungsroman* and a mock autobiography of a hero of the people, behind it is a sense of hurt. Trinidad is an impoverished colony where Hinduism decayed to a crude sense of ethnicity without any understanding of its philosophy and rituals. The black community, as represented by Mr Primrose, mimics white British behaviour to absurd extremes and seeks signs of racial prejudice.[15] The materials for personal and national advancement are not available. Most Indians still live in isolated rural communities, cut grass and sugar cane for a living, or own small shops. The ability to read and write is still rare. There is little opportunity for wealth except through owning land wanted by the oil companies. Bribery, drunkenness, violence and cynicism are common; religion, ethnic organizations and politics offer opportunities for personal advancement. This is a marooned, impoverished, disorganized, neglected colonial society which has been given a gift of elections.

There is in Naipaul's irony both brutality and amused admiration. Ganesh may be laughed at as he becomes G. Ramsay Muir but he is offered sympathetic interest, and his ability to remain independent and rise above circumstances is admirable. By contrast Indarsingh is treated with scorn. Naipaul has a Trinidadian delight in the con-man; he admires those who manage to succeed, those who seize the time and make use of opportunities. Better that than fail and make excuses.

Ganesh is the self-made hero of the classic nineteenth-century novel treated in terms of a backward society which offers few chances for advancement. Ganesh breaks all the rules, refuses to marry the woman his father chooses, quits his job as schoolteacher, and has a strong sense of himself as different and ordained for something larger than what is available in contemporary Trinidad. While it takes years for him to find a role, first as mystic masseur, then as politician, he is shrewd. He humiliates Ramlogan into paying for his survival until he can find a way to advance himself. Later, as a famous mystic he will control a fleet of taxis and a restaurant and receive part of the profits from materials sold to be used in rituals. He instinctively realizes that books and a general education will enable him to fulfil his ambitions.[16] He is a modernizer. He uses his reading in psychology and self-salesmanship to cure his patients. He not only makes himself, continually rewriting his history and taking new names and careers, he brings together the symbols and knowledge of the various cultures of Trinidad – Hindu, Moslem, Christian, modern, traditional. He even uses, according to circumstance, English, dialect, Hindi and a bit of Spanish. He offers an ironic, Trinidadian version of a rags-to-riches story. He is a hero of the people, an example of a people, especially Trinidadians of the Indian diaspora, remaking themselves, in ways that are necessarily crude, brutal, comic. The tone of the novel mixes attitudes of distaste, understanding, enjoyment, wonder and acceptance along with amusement.

Throughout the novel there are allusions to writing, books, book reviews and printing. If the novel shows how little understanding there is in Trinidad of literature, its genres and levels, the literary marketplace and the writer's career – and by implication why Naipaul had to leave Trinidad to become a writer – it also shows the need for self-definition through writing. Ganesh's writing is not only of poor quality and imitative, it is self-serving. No sooner does he write an autobiography than he suppresses it and abandons writing to pursue his political career. While at various stages in his life he uses narrative to make sense of himself and history, the lack of vocation and dedication leads him elsewhere.

The Suffrage of Elvira (1958) begins where *The Mystic Masseur* leaves off. The first novel sketches in the social history of Trinidad through the 1930s and 40s until the first election in 1946 under

universal adult franchise. Ganesh is representative of the first
generation of politicians, flamboyant individuals lacking political
parties and organizations. *The Suffrage of Elvira* concerns 1950 and
the 'second general election under universal adult franchise' when
'people began to see the possibilities' (p. 13). 'Possibilities' is
Naipaulian irony for the many ways people can gain, financially
and socially, from politics. The buying of blocks of votes from
leaders of ethnic communities, the paying for funerals, food and
drinks, was common practice in Trinidad at the time when Port of
Spain was known as the Sodom and Gomorrah of West Indian
politics.[17] But this is not the usual novel about third world post-
colonial corruption; it has none of the open anger, disillusionment and harsh satire of the novels of Chinua Achebe, Kwei
Armah or Wole Soyinka about the betrayal of ideals by politicians
and a corrupt society fighting over the spoils of independence.
Naipaul treats similar themes and portrays a similar process but his
manner is amusement at the social comedy. On the basis of what
he had learned about human nature within his large Indian family
he did not expect anything better to come from the political
process, and he has learned to hide his personal wounds. It is this
scepticism that distinguishes *The Suffrage of Elvira* from such a work
as V. S. Reid's *New Day* (1949). *New Day* is a nationalist novel which
sees elections as a step towards independence and is told in Jamai-
can English. Naipaul treats the granting of political power with
irony and scepticism as something the British wanted. Contrasted
to the lack of issues and open bribery for votes there is the 'Colonial Office documentary film about political progress in the colonies, the script of which was to be written, poetically, in London, by
a minor British poet' (p. 180).

   The Suffrage of Elvira is set in an isolated, neglected region, with
a large Indian population, rather than the more politically active
Negro and brown communities of urban Port of Spain. Blacks are
not central to the novel and the politics are between individuals
who are supposedly leaders of the Hindu and Moslem Indian
communities. There is no criticism of British rule by the narrator
or his characters, no overt ideological position; although there is
the implicit one that British electoral processes are a mimicry of
alien practices in such a community. The novel shows what Naipaul
in *A Middle Passage* describes as a picaroon society, a society without fixed rules in which humiliations and advancement are often
rapid and seemingly arbitrary, in which life can be brutal and in

which there are no ethical standards and cunning and conning are accepted and admired. 'Is my top. I thief it from a boy at school' (p. 74); '. . . you don't have to bribe them twice' (p. 132). It is assumed that bribery and seeking personal advantage is an accepted way of life. At the school polling station the clerk subjects the voters to long delays until Harbans gives him ten dollars. 'They visited warden, returning officer, poll clerks, policemen: a pertinacious but delicate generosity rendered these officials impartial' (p. 155). To prevent tampering with the ballot results you need 'men of tried criminality' (p. 186). At the conclusion the winners and losers are what individuals have gained and lost in relation to each other in the course of events connected to the election: 'Chittaranjan lost a son-in-law and Dhaniram lost a daughter-in-law. Elvira lost Lorkhoor and Lorkhoor won a reputation' (p. 207).

The novel portrays a people uninterested in ideas. Harbans is told early that if he does not purchase a van and loudspeaker for Baksh, 'you ain't got no Muslim vote' (p. 18). Similar sentiments are repeated, 'if you want my vote, you want my printery' (p. 73). We see a population so uneducated and ignorant that they need to be taught how to make an X on their ballot papers. Many changes in voting are influenced by superstition.

Trinidad in the novel is not yet a nation or people with demands and common assumptions beyond bribery and 'possibilities'. Candidates have no policies, represent no ideologies or classes. The incongruities of applying foreign notions to such a society can be seen in various incongruities of speech and action. The 'Epilogue: The Case of Whisky' offers a democratizing of the earlier 'possibilities' that Chitteranjan, Ramlogan and others saw in the electoral campaign. Now that Harbans is benefiting from his position on the Council, as shown by his double-breasted grey suit and new Jaguar, everyone wants some immediate personal benefit, some reward. People see the election as a chance for Harbans to get 'Five years' regular pay' and they want their share of the 'possibilities': 'they waste their good good time and they go and mark X on the vote-paper for your sake' (p. 200). '. . . Can't just come to a place and collect people good good vote and walk away' (p. 205).

In *The Suffrage of Elvira* people are types and seen from the outside with an emphasis on clothing and physical features ('He flashed his false teeth' [p. 16]) rather than psychologically. Character is fixed. Even at the end of the novel Baksh (whose name represents a bribe-like gift) finds new ways to get money from

Harbans. Chittaranjan, the one character to have dignity, is so true to his old-fashioned Hinduism that he gains nothing from the election and accepts without question that his daughter being seen briefly one night with a Muslim has sullied her reputation, which allows Harbans to get out of the agreement that his son will marry the daughter. So much for the promises of elected politicians! But that, Naipaul accepts, is the way of the world, especially in Trinidad.

Much of the novel is amusing social or literary comedy. There is Naipaul's concern with language in its various forms, whether Trinidadian expressions ('bacchanal') and grammar, Lorkhoor's inflated display of educated English ('begging you and imploring you and entreating you and beseeching you' [pp. 18–19]) which is imitated by Baksh (pp. 178, 191), misuse, amusing vulgarity ('Not only pee . . . He shake it' [p. 49]), insults ('piss-in-tail boy' [p. 81]), curses and threats ('I beat you till you pee' [p. 81]), or in various forms of play, 'down-couraged' (p. 37), and parody. Ramlogan is given a parody West Indian version of Shakespeare's Seven Ages of Man: 'When girl child small, they does crawl . . .' (p. 109). At the exact centre of the novel, a section which Naipaul uses to give emphasis, there is the humorous description of 'Dangerous' (p. 102) Tiger's walk through Elvira, a tongue-in-cheek parody by the author of the usual scene in the Hollywood Western where a tough gun slinger walks down the main street and is commented upon by frightened onlookers. 'Tiger came on, indifferent as sea or sky' (p. 103). Many scenes and speeches in the novel allude to, parody or seem based on films, as the cinema was the main cultural reference in Trinidad during Naipaul's youth.

The Suffrage of Elvira has a complicated plot, cluttered with incidents and many intertwined stories. While this is characteristic of the community plot developed around a specific situation, such as an election, that is common to third world novels in the early stages of decolonization, Naipaul is not at ease with the form. Such novels are usually an affirmation of communal values, a subculture or a colonized people – and their portrayal of a people is a political assertion. But Naipaul's point is rather the opposite. Here is an unhomogeneous assortment of peoples and cultures with nothing more in common than getting what they can out of a situation. The only character who has a complete ethical system, who lives by traditional values, is Chittaranjan, and he is one of the few losers connected with the election. His Brahminism is out-moded, unable to adapt to the free-for-all spoils that the bringing together of various cultures has produced in Trinidad. Naipaul's later novels will have a smaller cast of characters, focus on a few, have fewer events and will be less complicated in the action. They will be more Shakespearean in examining character within a society than a Ben Jonson Carnival with its whirl of many characters and multiplying plots. *The Suffrage of Elvira* is the last of Naipaul's entertainments, social comedies of the incongruities of colonial Trinidad: 'Things were crazily mixed up in Elvira. Everybody, Hindus, Muslims and Christians, owned a Bible; the Hindus and Muslims looking on it, if anything, with greater awe' (p. 66). With *A House for Mr Biswas* the comedy will be touched by anger, involvement, remembered scars. There will be less distance and pretence of amused detachment.

3

A House for Mr Biswas and The Middle Passage

A *House for Mr Biswas* (1961), Naipaul's first major novel, belongs with such classics of the new English literatures as Patrick White's *Voss* and Chinua Achebe's *Things Fall Apart* in which through the portrayal of an individual the complexities and aspirations of a previously ignored colonial or colonized culture are articulated, given epic, mythic stature. Similar to these two novels, it is an imaginative, fictional recreation of the past. The main characters, places and events are based on Naipaul's father, Naipaul's own youth and the larger family of which they were a part (see Appendix A).

Although the manner remains comic, Naipaul develops some of the major themes that recur in his fiction and which might be described as his vision of life. Towards the centre of *A House for Mr Biswas*, Anand, Mr Biswas' son and second child, surprisingly decides to remain at his father's incompletely built house at Green Vale although his pregnant mother, after brutality by her husband, flees to Hanuman House with her other children. Biswas has become mentally unstable through undernourishment, solitude and the harshness of his life. Abandoned by his family, trapped in a loveless marriage, poor and unable to get a foot up the ladder of life, Biswas fears being murdered by the resentful estate workers he supervises; his angry, irrational behaviour towards his wife is the start of a nervous breakdown. When he asks his son, who has lived until now at Hanuman House, why he stays with him, Anand replies 'Because they was going to leave you alone' (p. 279). After Biswas' dog is horribly murdered, Anand wants to leave but is delayed by his father, who can no longer face solitude.

Besides being threatened by the workers Biswas is also threat-

ened by the natural world. A terrible storm begins. Winged ants
invade the house, bite Anand and soon die. A column of fire ants
appear and soon capture and cart off the winged ants. Anand
hears human voices outside the house which he and his father
think are those of dismissed workers planning to harm them. The
wind and torrential rain worsen; the roof shakes, some of the
corrugated sheets are torn off or flap dangerously. The house
seems likely to collapse. There is thunder, lightning, the wind
blows out the lamp and 'when the lightning went out the room was
part of the black void' (p. 292). Anand screams and screams as the
wind sweeps through the now floorless, wall-less house until he
sees a man carrying a hurricane lamp and a cutlass. It is a labourer
from the barracks looking for a lost calf. The lamp illuminates a
'wet chaos' (p. 293); but Anand and Biswas are now saved, although the latter has temporarily lost his mind and does not know
where he is or what has happened.

The biblical echoes are less of the rainbow after the flood than
a return to the beginning of time before the creation, an unmaking,
a decreation, of the protection, comforts and order offered by
civilization and society. In the Green Vale chapter the protections
of society are removed until Biswas and Anand are isolated, helpless against the violence of others and the natural world. They are
reduced to the condition of the insects who are defenceless against
the attack of organized groups of other insects. Nature is uncaring,
dangerous; life is short; creatures are naturally at war with each
other and protected only by being part of a community. Biswas'
fear of harm and death is also a fear of extinction, annihilation,
the void. The void is in his mind, a kind of insanity in which his
selfhood and individuality are lost. The stripping away of the
physical comforts and protections of civilization results in a loss of
rationality, humanity, other kinds of consciousness than fear. He is
metamorphosed into something primitive, subhuman. Although
supposedly a rationalist he chants a mantra for protection. The
chaos of Biswas' life has brought mental disorder. Such fears have
now been transmitted to his son.

Here is the central vision that finds expression in Naipaul's
language of order, disorder, extinction, void, and which influences the way he looks at society, politics and culture. The world is
without purpose, violent, dangerous; in the natural world life is
fearful, comfortless, irrational and brutal. Creatures organize societies for self-protection, they cooperate to assure essentials such as

food and to build homes for comfort and refuge. While the effectiveness of societies to provide for their members differs, anyone
outside society is likely to become a victim of the void. Well-
organized societies with large resources and the ability to use their
resources are most likely to resist extinction and to provide superior opportunities for their citizens. Achievement, whether
through writing, building or empire, is a way of leaving a mark on
history, a way of avoiding annihilation and the void; it is a way of
becoming more than the short-lived flying ant carried away for
food by the fire ants.

Behind the scene of Biswas' mental collapse during the hurricane are events in Naipaul's own life, events to which he has often
alluded. There is his father's mental breakdown, symbolized by
looking into a mirror and not seeing his own reflection, which led
to a withdrawal from the family. His father's mental condition
affected Naipaul; he suffered from a similar breakdown at Oxford
and there are suggestions in his writings of other periods of
depression. The unsettled period of Naipaul's own childhood,
moving houses, living among relatives, is reflected in Biswas' story
as, probably, are fears for the future of the Indians in Trinidad and
the insecurities of his early period as a writer in London. Houses,
gardens and family gatherings are often symbols in Naipaul's
novels because they represent order, society, civilization,
achievement or at least their potential or ideal even when actually
disillusioning.

But to see the storm scene at the centre of *A House for Mr Biswas*
only in regard to its themes, metaphysics, symbols and autobiographical significances ignores its clear relationship to the tempest
in Shakespeare's *King Lear*. Biswas brings to mind Lear, unhoused,
rejected by his family, alone with the Fool, unprotected from the
violence of nature. Lear's madness is not only the result of the
storm; it has a history in his foolishness and self-destructive anger
as well as the harsh behaviour of others. Both the novel and the
play are about individuals who thought they could stand on their
own and find that once they are unhoused, powerless, outside
society, madness follows.

Both the novel and the play are concerned with angry, self-
destructive fathers, the father's preference for one child (Biswas'
for his eldest daughter Savi) over others, the tearing of family
bonds, the surprising love of a rejected child for the father and the
father's eventual recognition of that affection. The way Biswas'

emotional turmoil is reflected in the symbolism of tempestuous nature as well as a response to the harsh reality of nature is indebted to Shakespeare's technique in *King Lear*. Throughout the novel there are literary echoes which foreshadow the parallels of the storm scene. The prologue concludes: 'How terrible it would have been . . . to have lived and died as one had been born, unnecessary and unaccommodated' (pp. 13–14).[18] Biswas is Shakespeare's poor unaccommodated man. His often repeated chant from schooldays that 'ought oughts are ought' is a version of 'nothing will come of nothing'.

Naipaul builds his fiction on models and the Lear model helps him to universalize his story, contributes to the metaphysical dimension of the novel in which nature is treated as alien, uncaring, and in which people must existentially create their own significance by their actions. The parallels recall in *King Lear* the importance of society, of nurture as opposed to raw nature. This provides a perspective on such themes in the novel as the need for education, civilization, achievement, rationality and charity (love of others; helping others). The family drama is also universalized. History becomes a story of blind, self-destructive, angry fathers, misjudged children, the need for love, for emotional as well as material protection.

Just as an individual cannot prosper without a supporting society, so art needs foundations in earlier art. Just as it is impossible for Biswas to find the resources to build a house in his circumstances in Trinidad, so he lacks suitable literary models. He reads books of self-improvement that have no relevance to his life, he hears avant garde poetry of a complexity that he cannot master and which is foreign to his circumstances. The only model who is mentioned which seems appropriate to Biswas' society is Dickens, the Dickens of grotesques and the Dickens of those who struggle to survive and to find a place in their world while needing emotional satisfaction. Anand's liking for Dickens points to the Dickenesque characteristics of *A House for Mr Biswas*.

There is a radical difference between King Lear and Mr Biswas. Rather than a king foolishly giving away his power and possessions, Biswas is poor, without social position and has no possessions. He cannot even 'claim' his children. Such inversions of the situations in his literary models are common to Naipaul's writings. They are part of his allusive ironies. The ironies insist upon the differences between societies he writes about and the societies of his literary models. Lear has possessions and accommodations from which he foolishly dispossesses himself, whereas beginning with his birth Mr Biswas is unaccommodated. Lear disorders his society; Biswas is born into a disorderly society, has temporary places of refuge, such as with Pundit Jairam, Bhandat's rum shop and Hanuman House, but must create his own order, symbolized by having his own house. That he dies unemployed, with the badly built house mortgaged and two of his children in foreign lands, shows that his world is still only partly ordered, and that the disorder that began with the immigration of indentured Indian labour to Trinidad is still in process, the journey still unfinished, the diaspora still unsettled.

With such differences between Lear's world and Biswas' their narratives cannot be similar. *King Lear* ends with the restoration of order through a new order. *A House for Mr Biswas* begins on an upbeat mood of celebration but concludes with 'empty house'. Just the way Biswas' Sikkim Street house has been built from various materials which the contractors found here and there, so Naipaul mixes Trinidadian social history with a large variety of European and American literary models and allusions ranging from the Bible to books by James Joyce and Marcel Proust to create a novel unlike those of Europe.[19]

Just as Trinidadian is unlike English society, and a West Indian house will be dissimilar to a British house, so *A House for Mr Biswas* cannot be like *Mansfield Park* or *Howard's End*. The material conditions are different, there is no house or national cultural tradition to inherit. *A House for Mr Biswas* could be read as an allegory of the painful progress of the major group among the Trinidadian Indians, Hindu northern Indians, to build a house on an island which still feels alien, unwelcoming and without the likely materials for a home. Each house Biswas inhabits, builds or owns is figurative of the condition of his situation and that of the Trinidadian Indians of the time. They range from the enclosed security of Hanuman House, the village shops in which the owners live, the unfinished attempts to build simple houses in the country to the half-modern, partly owned house of Sikkim Street. *A House for Mr Biswas* provides a social history of the community. Brought to Trinidad as indentured labourers to replace the freed black slaves, the Indians were isolated, worked on the sugar cane estates, reformed their traditional culture, even reconstituting castes, pinched pennies to purchase small plots of farming land and became owners of rum shops and small general stores. Later some invested in taxi cabs, became merchants or became wealthy when oil deposits were found on their land. It was not until the Second World War, when Americans built a national highway, that there were sufficient new opportunities, new money and modern roads for the Indians to move from the country to Port of Spain and begin their still uneasy accommodation with the urban, predominantly black and mixed creole population. As Trinidad moved towards self-government education became important; there were new, if limited, opportunities for employment.

At first there was little education available to Indians. Rural schools could not, and still often cannot, prepare pupils for the entrance examination to secondary schools in Port of Spain. Only Port of Spain offered proper tuition for the examinations. The secondary schools were expensive and at the time Anand was in primary school, only a few scholarships were available through competitive national examinations. Until 1970 anyone who had graduated from secondary school would have to go abroad for professional or university training. For those who could not afford it, only four government scholarships were available to study abroad. Urban whites and blacks were obviously best placed to use education for advancement.

Biswas' story is both representative of the history of the Trinidadian East Indian and a special case. The history of the Trinidadian Asian Indian could be put together from aspects of his life and the lives of those to whom he was related by birth and marriage. Yet no one single character in the novel can be said to be typical of the Trinidadian Indian; Naipaul avoids the simplifications, falsifications and dishonest sentimentality of protest fiction with its typical characters and illustrative plots supposedly representative of a community. Lives, situations and people differ. Some have luck, others do not. Some destroy their chances, others seize the day. Biswas' older brothers as children become workers on the cane fields and never have the opportunity to learn to read or write; after his father dies and the family is dispersed, Biswas is sent to school by his aunt. Biswas foolishly marries and becomes a Tulsi, thus losing the favour of his rich aunt Tara; this becomes an opportunity for Bhandat's children.

A House for Mr Biswas, like most of Naipaul's fiction, is both an investigation of society and a story of discrete, differing, individual lives. Impoverished, living in rural Trinidad, Biswas could never be an inventor; there would not be the materials, the books, the supporting culture and opportunities. He could not be a writer. He would not be familiar with contemporary models, have other writers to help him or have access to a market. Biswas lives in an impoverished colonial society in which most people do not read, education is not easily available, English is not always used for conversations, literary models come from abroad and are inappropriate for local society. Literature, therefore, seems dead, part of the European past. There is little literary culture in which to learn, develop or operate. Biswas learns to write clear prose as a reporter and for a time there is a market for lively journalism; but when the newspaper's policy changes, even that tiny literary marketplace comes to an end.

When Biswas attempts to write fiction he cannot imagine his own life as providing material, unlike Anand who, ignoring the British examples of what a day at the seashore should be like, writes a excellent composition at school describing the time he almost drowned at the beach. Instead of honestly making use of his personal experience Biswas writes and rewrites a fantasy about not being married and loving a young, thin, woman who is unable to have children; literature for him is the opposite of his actual life. Significantly he writes two versions of the story, one with a handsome white hero, the other with an unattractive brown or Indian male character. Since the novels he reads are often romances about white handsome Englishmen and since he lives in a culture in which to be white and English is to be superior, his imagination follows such conventions. When he writes of Indians he sees ugliness, his own condition; there is as yet no local literary tradition which will allow him to write realistically about someone like himself. Although there were some earlier predecessors, such as the short stories of Naipaul's own father, *A House for Mr Biswas* is one of the first Indian Trinidadian novels, the beginning of such a tradition.

Biswas' need for a house and family is partly psychological, as a result of early homelessness, lack of a father and need for mothering. (When Biswas is expelled from Pundit Jairam's house and returns to his mother expecting welcome and comfort 'instead of being pleased to see him . . . her manner was harsh . . . she shouted at him' [p. 57].) But he is also the equivalent of the orphan or fatherless hero of the European novel who comes to the capital city to conquer. Biswas wants to impress, to achieve, to make his mark on the world, to rise above his birth and circumstances. And he does so, although in a limited way, by going to Port of Spain, by becoming a locally famous journalist, by working for the government, by bringing together his family and asserting himself as head of the family, by contributing to Anand's education, by gaining his wife's trust, by owning a car and purchasing a house.

For someone of his background and lack of opportunities Biswas' progress is epic. Through will, chance and changing circumstances his life has evolved from homelessness, dependency on others, poverty, lack of a recognized place in the world (his birth was not even officially recorded) to a homeowner, head of a family, a father with two children who are studying abroad. He has created a place for himself in the new world in contrast to the futile poverty to which he appeared destined as a child. The novel is a celebration of his achievement (and the achievement of the Trinidadian Indian). This achievement is dissimilar to that of the classic novels and epics in the distance Biswas has had to travel from the world of the rural Indian peasant to a semblance of New World middle-class success. At times he has luck. Ramkhilawan, searching for his calf, discovers Biswas and Anand during the storm; Ramchand allows Biswas to stay with him in Port of Spain; Mr Burnett, amused by Biswas' personality, is willing to give him a trial period as a reporter. Such chance encounters are important to Biswas and more likely in the city than the country.

If *A House for Mr Biswas* is a celebration of Biswas' success (a half-success since this is a half-made society which cannot offer more opportunity), and the immense pains such an achievement required in the circumstances, it is also a story of individual will. Lives are limited by circumstance, they are also willed. Naipaul claims that the European novel is about will and achievement in contrast to traditional Indian fatalism and passivity. Biswas' parents are fatalistic, passive, repressive of desire and ambition. Their traditional Indian philosophy is suitable for the bare survival offered by the rural impoverished life they know. But when the family falls apart and Biswas is on his own, except for the help of his aunt Tara, he must strive to survive, unlike his mother who depressively comments that perhaps it would be better if he killed himself.

The Tulsi family into which he marries appears to offer protection. Hanuman House is initially described as looking like a fortress; but Hanuman House is not a solid, evolving society, it is a

temporary refuge for those by circumstances or personality unable
to find a place in Trinidad. Rather than Hanuman House typifying
Indian traditional culture, the Tulsi children go to Christian
missionary schools, the husbands of Tulsi daughters live with
the wife's family (instead of bringing the daughters to their own
family as is customary in India) and there is an absurd mixture of
Westernization and ritualism. The makeshift, temporary nature of
this small enclosed, self-protective community is revealed by its
rapid disintegration, when the war brought more opportunities
for Indians to acquire the skills and means to enter the wider
community. It was for Biswas a long-drawn-out time of futile rebellion, of not knowing what to do, before his journey to Port of
Spain, a place where there were better opportunities for employment, a chance to make his mark on the world and save money to
buy a house. Naipaul associates rural life with poverty and the city
with opportunity.

   Biswas' rebellion against the Tulsis and his circumstances was
bound to fail while limited by Hanuman House, The Chase or
Green Vale. Without money, power, skills or available employment
for which he could develop skills, his Westernized sense of self, of
individuality, was bound to be frustrated. He can only be an absurd
rebel, someone who attempts to paddle his own canoe without a
canoe or water. And, of course, he is partly to blame. Like many of
Naipaul's characters he becomes intoxicated by love and foolishly
marries. When he does not demand a dowry for his marriage and
does not have the strength of character to demand that the Tulsis
provide him with a future career, he ruins his chances with his
Aunt Tara. Fearing humiliation, not knowing where to turn for
guidance, he trusts appearances, even buying the Sikkim Street
house without properly examining it or comparing it with what
else he could purchase for the same price.

   Biswas is, like many of Naipaul's central characters, a rebel, an
outsider, even, when he has some money, a bit of a dandy. He is an
impoverished West Indian version of the modern rebel. The first
part of the novel shows such rebellion is futile for those still in the
condition of near slavery without the means of self-support. Biswas
can only taunt and insult those upon whom he is dependent. In
contrast to Biswas' rebellion his wife Shama remains closely attached to the Tulsi family, accepting pressures to conform. Tulsi
House is a hierarchical feudal society with Mrs Tulsi and her two
sons the royalty. Although suitable roles are found for those who

conform, such as Hari who becomes family priest and pundit, everyone except the mother and her two sons are treated as dependants.

Just the way the Indians of Trinidad tried to reconstruct a social order of caste and such customs as the thread ceremony and arranged marriages in Trinidad only to find them challenged (as, for example, by the way Ramchand goes to Port of Spain and prospers) or ridiculous in the New World, so Hanuman House is an attempt at preserving orthodoxy built on unorthodox foundations. It provides temporary security at the cost of denying Western individuality and will. Afterwards everyone will be part of the individualistic, competitive new world in which advancement often depends upon educational qualifications, personal will and the willingness to take chances.

The fragmentation of the Tulsis into nuclear families, each with its own house, is also, as shown in the novel, the beginning of a process of social transformation in which there will be more intermarriages between Hindus and Christians, friendships will be based on class and occupation rather than family, and children will go abroad for education and sometimes not return to Trinidad. The temporary reconstructed rural traditional Indian Hindu world represented by the Tulsis has largely disappeared by the end of the novel but not been replaced with another ordered society. While Indians and creoles now live and work together there is little evidence from the novel of assimilation.

In *A House for Mr Biswas* freedom is a mixed blessing. Both individual and political freedom require the material, emotional and intellectual resources to avoid continuing dependency and the childish self-destructive outbursts that result when desires cannot be fulfilled. Biswas was always free to leave the Tulsis, to have a home, to establish his family, but he lacked the material resources. While his failures were personal they also resulted from a society unable to provide opportunities for education, employment, savings, investment, rewards.

The novel shows an impoverished, disorganized Trinidad and implicitly criticizes imperialism for having created such a mess in which those of African and Indian descent have been brought together without the resources to live or make better lives. Looked at this way, while Naipaul is one of many writers from the former colonies who have criticized colonialism and who see their lands and people as victims of the Empire, he is not a simple-minded

nationalist who believes that local cultural assertion and cries of
victimization will provide a solution to the problems left by history.
Trinidad in *A House for Mr Biswas* lacks the resources required for
authentic independence. As Biswas discovers when he attempts to
find employment or build his house, freedom can be dangerous,
humiliating and self-defeating. Biswas' situation is that of the colony,
his own attempts at independence are limited by the condition of
the society into which he is born; frustrated self-assertion turns
into self-destructive rage, the tempest that temporarily disorders
Biswas' mind.

While *A House for Mr Biswas* is a study of West Indian society, a
record of the Asian Indians in Trinidad and an imaginative reconstruction of the life of Naipaul's father, it is also in part an autobiographical novel about the relationship between father and son and
about how the author of the novel became what he is. It is a version
of the many late nineteenth- and early twentieth-century novels
offering a fictionalized autobiography, a portrait of the artist as a
young man, a remembrance of things past. Its originality is its
unusual use of a modern European literary genre for totally different circumstances – in which the usual developing awareness of a
young person's moral growth is replaced by Anand's increasing
consciousness of the harsh conditions which made his father and
himself. The novel has an unusual double focus beginning with
Biswas but from the middle onwards increasingly split between
father and son.

There is an unusual remark by the narrator after Myna is born
which anticipates the author's later involvement with Anand's
perspective: 'Anand (asleep on the bed: no more rubbing for him,
for the rest of his life)' (p. 195). While this is an example of the
theme of the loss of protection and motherly care that is part of
growing up, a theme often found in Naipaul's novels, it also looks
forward to the ways Anand will respond to the harshness and
insecurities of his life. 'Anand had a moment of alarm when he got
up. His pillowcase, lying at the foot of his bedding on the floor,
looked empty' (p. 214). Such narration either sees the world
through Anand's eyes or is more sympathetic to him than to other
characters. 'He cleaned the tub, and it was such a perfectly made
thing he would have liked to keep it.' (p. 335). There is an obvious
joke when Anand's enemy during the time he is preparing for the
scholarship examinations is a pampered 'simpering, lip-licking'
(p. 471) fool named Vidiadhar, Naipaul's own first name. When-

ever Vidiadhar appears the narrator drops his distance: 'The little thug' (p. 474); 'his crapaud-foot handwriting' (p. 491); 'This was a lie. Vidiadhar didn't even know the meaning of the words. He just liked their sound' (p. 543).

A House for Mr Biswas is, among its varied themes, about becoming a writer and how the book itself came into being. Biswas' sense of humour and parody makes him into a excellent, if limited, popular feature writer for his newspaper, but he cannot find the distance from his own experience to turn it into art. He keeps leaving unfinished a story which is about the life he wished he had. Anand, however, after he almost drowns, writes directly from his own experience: 'But in this last composition there were no dashes and repetitions; no hampers, no motorcars, no golden arcs of sand. . . . The composition ended with a denunciation of the sea' (p. 357). Naipaul, like Derek Walcott, often associates the sea with disorder, danger, the violence of nature and death. His Caribbean is not an exotic paradise for tourists.

Throughout the novel the reader is aware of the author as literary critic: 'once [Biswas] had got a slant and an opening sentence everything followed. Sentence generated sentence, paragraph led to paragraph, and his articles had a flow and a unity' (p. 375). 'He had no words to say what he wanted to say, the poet's words, which held more than the sum of their meaning. . . . He did not think of rhythm; he used no cheating abstract words' (p. 484). In contrast to the bad writers, most of whom imitate British subject matter and attitudes inappropriate to Trinidad, while not knowing how to transform their models into local art, Anand both writes from his own experience and adapts Dickens' London to his own world. He writes in his diary: 'This is the worst Christmas Day I have ever spent; . . . I feel like Oliver Twist in the workhouse' (p. 394).

Here is the explanation of Naipaul's inner world and his ironic manner. When the Tulsi children 'spent so much time away from the house, they formed a community of their own, outside family laws. No one ruled; there were only the weak and the strong' (pp. 411–12). 'Though no one recognized his strength, Anand was among the strong. His satirical sense kept him aloof . . . satire led to contempt, and . . . contempt, quick, deep, inclusive, became part of his nature. It led to inadequacies, to self-awareness and a lasting loneliness. But it made him unassailable' (pp. 412–13). Earlier we are told while 'political books' left Mr Biswas 'feeling more helpless and more isolated than ever' (p. 374) he found 'solace' in the novels of Dickens. 'In the grotesques of Dickens everything he feared and suffered from was ridiculed and diminished, so that his own anger, his own contempt became unnecessary.' 'He shared his discovery with Anand.' 'Anand understood. Father and son, each saw the other as weak and vulnerable' (p. 374).

The descriptions of Anand help towards an understanding of Naipaul's distanced manner in his writing, his sense of irony, his judgements of falsity and pretence, his lack of sentimentality, his instinct for *picong* (attack), his attitude of superiority, his appreciation of success, his love of paradox and of acting an extreme version of whatever he is accused of by his critics. Naipaul has said that his view of the world was formed while young, living in a large family. Naipaul's literary and public personality has other characteristics than those given Anand, but anyone wanting to understand what made Naipaul what he is might keep Anand in mind. Biswas needing to keep his job during the *Sentinel*'s new policy of sobriety finds himself 'on the side of the grotesque' (p. 375). Naipaul usually keeps himself on the other side whether the dominating 'grotesques' are on the political right or left, whether of the first or third world.

Several times in the novel we are told how Anand learns about his parents' past. Naipaul is concerned to establish for the reader how this text came into existence, its basis in reality, and how Anand, the implied author, came into possession of the facts he recounts. Just as the early eighteenth-century novel must establish its credentials as fictionalized truth (rather than pure invention, lies) so a novel about a previously unmapped social territory and people such as the Trinidad Indians must justify its authenticity.

Naipaul needs to establish such confidence and seems to be uncomfortable with the distance between fiction and the reality of personal experience upon which it is based. In his novels we are often aware of his conscious insertion of the narrator into the story, of his need to justify why what we are reading is there and how it came into being. Naipaul interpolates such information as Biswas telling the children about himself or Anand accidentally finding some old letters written to his mother. Events in Biswas' life and the acquisition of property are often dated by the mention of events in Europe. Local history, which was previously formless, without an established chronology, must first be placed in the perspective of an established history, such as that of modern Europe, before it can be organized, found significant and begin to stand on its own.

In such an unsettled society, where the family has no records and lacks associations with the land, buildings, important events, achievements or a rooted community, history is a mystery which must be imagined from the little that is known, discovered or felt to be representative. Narrative creates an order where there was previously only disorder and the loss of the past; the novel rescues from the void Naipaul's family history and that of the Asian Trinidadian Indian community. Art, as narrative and as achievement, provides a voice for the previously unvoiced, creates a place in the world for those unaccommodated, as did Naipaul's Sikkim Street house. Biswas' house, even Hanuman House, now belongs to the same order as Mansfield Park, Howard's End, Brideshead, Pembroke House. It has become part of the new literary and cultural tradition of English and world literature.

There is an explicit analogy between the order provided by houses and art. 'Soon it seemed to the children that they had never lived anywhere but in the tall square house in Sikkim Street. From now their lives would be ordered, their memories coherent' (p. 581). The past is soon forgotten, but Anand, homesick, troubled and lonely at university in England sometimes recalls the past and 'later, and very slowly, in securer times of different stresses, when the memories had lost the power to hurt, with pain or joy, they would fall into place and give back the past' (p. 581).

While Anand is imagined writing the novel as a means of regaining the past the reader understands Anand as figurative of Naipaul. Although many novelists have used a similar convention to distance their life from their fiction, Naipaul's clear identification with Anand keeps collapsing the distance, allowing the autobiographical to emerge more than is usual in such writing. 'And now Mr Biswas needed his son's interest and anger. In all the world there was no one else to whom he could complain. . . Anand said he wanted to come home. . . . But the plan fell through; Anand changed his mind' (p. 588). The story will be continued years later in *The Enigma of Arrival* which might be considered the second half of *A House for Mr Biswas*, although from the perspective of autobiographical fiction, if one allows for its greater inventiveness, *The Mimic Men* is the middle volume of the trilogy, three novels which would need to be supplemented with *An Area of Darkness* and

'Prologue to an Autobiography' to fill in significant parts of the story.

A House for Mr Biswas can be seen as layered upon an autobiographical foundation over which are the stories of Mr Biswas, the Tulsis, the Trinidadian Indians and even a record of change in Trinidad over the past fifty years, changes which are placed in the context of modern history. Rather than 'a place that was nowhere, a dot on the map of the island, which was a dot on the map of the world' (p. 237), Green Vale and the other places in the novel are given a thereness and put on the map of modern history, a history seen, however, in the context of the Indian diaspora rather than the slave trade. The need for literary models to build upon is seen in that sentence about 'a dot on the map of the island' which inverts a passage in *A Portrait of the Artist as a Young Man.*

A House for Mr Biswas is a carefully constructed novel. I have written in detail elsewhere about how artistic order is imposed through such techniques as a tightly controlled formal structure, parallel events, recurring images and phrases, even tightly knit rhetorical and sound patterns.[20] The book is consciously interwoven with such motifs as houses, gardens, Christmas, jobs, possessions, attempts at writing, historical allusions, dates, clothes, records of the past, money, education and literature. The novel has fifteen sections consisting of a prologue, an epilogue, and a chronology which is divided into two parts of equal length, the first part of six sections, the second of seven sections. The first half of the novel is set in rural areas and is concerned with Biswas' futile attempts in such circumstances to better his condition and gain the material foundations for a modern life of individualism, personal possessions, intimacy and the nuclear family. The second half is mostly set in Port of Spain and shows the more exciting life and opportunities of the city; better jobs are available, the various races and cultures begin to mix, people are more in touch with and affected by the world outside Trinidad. Time speeds up. This two-part structure, which Naipaul will use again in other works, is an expansion of his methods in 'Man-man' where the first half of the story seemed a group of rather pointless events as Man-man scratched around for means to support himself and pass the time; then the death of Man-man's dog brings this period to an end as it forces him to find other means of survival. The second half of the story has more continuity and development and involves the community when he becomes a preacher and begins his imitation of

Christ. In both the story and the novel Naipaul makes use of parallel events and phrases between the two halves.

Just as the epilogue recalls the prologue in scene, phrases and events, so many sections of the novel recall earlier pages. For example the father's funeral in the first chapter, which results in Biswas losing his home and the break up of his immediate family, is recalled with a difference by the book's conclusion when Biswas, now a homeowner and head of a family, is buried. The first half of the novel is itself circular with the scene of Biswas' mental break-down during the storm at Green Vale bringing to mind such events in section I as the threatening men outside the family hut looking for money and the drowned calf. Outside Hanuman House Biswas' life at The Chase and Green Vale recalls the village and life at the estate at the start of the novel. Indeed Biswas is at the end of Part I no better off than when he left his mother and started to seek employment. He is jobless, without money, without a home, without a family he can call his own.

When he goes to Port of Spain at the beginning of Part II he brings to mind his earlier innocent attempts to find employment and the role of sign-painting in his life; sign-painting brought him to the Tulsis and marriage, later it helps him towards a chance to become a reporter. Some other obvious parallels in the novel are the way Anand's humiliation about his bowel movements at school recalls Biswas' disgrace at Pundit Jairam's house; Govind's beating of Biswas (p. 135) is recalled in the description of his reconcilia-tion with Biswas (p. 557). The fifteen years of Biswas' life and the rapid social changes in Port of Spain usually reverse similar events during the thirty-one years in the countryside in Part I. When Biswas and his children are humiliated at Hanuman House there is no one to protect them, no place worthwhile to which they can go. When in Part II Anand is humiliated and Mrs Tulsi tells Biswas to leave, there seems, because of the housing shortage, no place they can go, but a house is found and purchased. Whereas in Part I (I.3) Hanuman House seems an ordered, protective Indian for-tress, although aesthetically ugly and suffocating for individual aspirations, the lovely French estate house at Shorthills (which in section II.2 is structurally parallel to Hanuman House) reveals the collapse of Tulsi order; it is unable to protect its inhabitants and is plundered for individual gain. At Shorthills the Tulsis have no social position and are exotic outsiders in a creolized community; symbolically they have moved from the rural Indian world to the outskirts of the urbanized part African, part French, part Spanish nation. And their destruction of the house and its gardens could be seen as an allegory of how the new society that was coming into being during the war will in its ignorance, opportunism and ruthless ways destroy the few graces left from the colonial past. Both Indian and creolized French traditions will crumble before the rush to be part of the Americanized world which followed the Second World War.

After writing *A House for Mr Biswas* Naipaul was offered a grant to return to Trinidad where the head of the government, Eric Williams, suggested that he write a book of reportage and observation about the Caribbean. *The Middle Passage* (1962) is the first of his travel books. Naipaul's books, especially his early books, are based upon literary models and his model was that of a European traveller to the colonies. Only after more experience could Naipaul create his own form and manner for such books. He adopts the manner of a Victorian travel writer to examine Trinidad, British Guiana, Surinam, Martinique and Jamaica. His specific model is James Anthony Froude, a writer intensely critical both of the crude philistinism of the British settlers and the culture of other peoples. The model strengthens the claims that the basic situation in the region has not changed since the last century; the Europeans created no worthwhile society or culture, established no lasting economic foundations, had no vision, but imported as slaves and labourers large numbers of people from different cultures whom they discriminated against and then abandoned to their mutual antagonism without providing means of improving their situation.

Mimicry of the colonizer, racial resentment, envy, political fantasy and violence are the result and can be expected to intensify with self-government unless the region can overcome ethnic differences in a positive nationalism and develop cultural pride.

> I had seen how deep in nearly every West Indian, high and low, were the prejudices of race; how often these prejudices were rooted in self contempt. . . . Everyone spoke of nation and nationalism but no one was willing to surrender the privileges or even the separateness of his group. Nowhere . . . was there any binding philosophy. . . . With an absence of a feeling of community, there was an absence of pride, and there was even cynicism . . . the race conflicts of every territory were growing sharper. (pp. 253–4)

The nationalism of *The Middle Passage* seems the usual fare of the independence era of the early 1960s and should have been unexceptional. But Naipaul hurt feelings in bringing attention to racial conflicts and prejudices, offering dismissive summaries of the region's history, and criticizing the existing culture. Some found offensive such remarks as, 'For nothing was created in the British West Indies, no civilization as in Spanish America, no great revolution as in Haiti or the American colonies' (p. 27). The essays are influenced by Naipaul's anxieties in returning to the Caribbean, his place of origins which he had fled and rejected. 'I knew Trinidad to be unimportant, uncreative, cynical . . . Power was recognized, but dignity was allowed to no one. Every person of eminence was held to be crooked and contemptible. We live in a society which denied itself heroes' (p. 43). Many of the problems raised by Naipaul are still relevant; but as they were expressed without the usual rhetoric of black–white conflict, victimization and cultural assertion, they became uncomfortable: 'Colonialism distorts the identity of the subject people, and the Negro in particular is bewildered and irritable. Racial equality and assimilation are attractive but only underline the loss, since to accept assimilation is in a way to accept permanent inferiority' (p. 181).

The increasing racial conflict between blacks and Indians in British Guiana, and the example of the Martinique Indians who had lost knowledge of their culture, heightened his feelings about the insecure place of the Asian Indians in the West Indies. In the West Indies 'nationalism is the only revitalizing force' (p. 153), but British Guiana instead of having 'an ordered and overdue social revolution' had split into its 'component parts', a dangerous situation brought about by 'racial rivalry' and fear. As Naipaul became more analytical, better informed, and more experienced of the wider world, he came to see that such notions were simplistic; he added a note prefacing later editions of *The Middle Passage* saying that if he had understood that he was writing about the 'problems of a client culture and a client economy' he would have been 'less romantic about the healing power, in such a culture, of political or racial assertion'.

4

Mr Stone and the Knights Companion and An Area of Darkness

Naipaul's first phase consisted of four works of fiction and a travel book about the Caribbean in which his manner is amused or satiric. His second phase comprises two novels set in England, a travel book about India and a history of early Trinidad. His manner is more serious and there is an increasing attraction to and resistance against traditional Indian passivity and fatalism. His year in India marked a major crisis in his life by revealing there could be no return to his origins, but in England he continued to feel a colonial outsider in exile from the political disorder of the decolonizing third world. Feeling unsettled, unrooted, he began questioning his life and the life of being a writer. What was to be his subject matter and his relationship to English literature? What was he really writing about – society, his past, himself, the artist, the world, the relationship of art to what? Now that England and India had failed as homes could he return to Trinidad despite its preoccupation with race? Because of such concerns the novels become more densely layered, with a variety of significances, many levels of meaning, ranging from the autobiographical to the philosophical.

Naipaul carries his obsessions with him and they reappear unexpectedly. The same concerns recur, usually enriched with further insight and complications, but are seldom settled. From early on until the present he will feel the need for freedom, activity, achievement, will and individuality and this will often start in some act of rebellion, some departure from routine and security. A novel will tell the story of a struggle for self-assertion, its excitements, rages,

54

passion, problems, irritations, defeats, and conclude, sometimes triumphantly, sometimes with frustration, with ambivalence towards the worth of the struggle. This may seem strange from an author who sees the novel as celebrating Western man's assertion of will within society, an existential making of one's self and one's place in an otherwise meaningless world, but throughout the novels there are other attitudes and philosophical positions. One is deterministic. Individuals are limited in their possibilities by their society and their material circumstances. Naipaul keeps questioning the worth of the struggle to achieve and leave a mark on the world. Is it worth the pain of separation from the security of group and routine, especially as desires and hopes are seldom realized in the way expected? This notion of the vanity of human wishes may be the result of personal experience, but it is expressed in ways which suggest a traditional Indian view in which desire, activity and change are the world of illusion, of unnecessary pain.

Whereas the Hindu can hope to be released from the world of illusion through contemplation, acceptance and eventual return to the One, Naipaul's world is secular, his cosmos that of Western science, and death is final, an annihilation of the self, not a stage in a history of reincarnations, not some ultimate peace of non-being. If death is tempting as withdrawal from pain, it is also the end of feeling, of consciousness, of the self. History teaches one form of transcendence in achievements, the monuments of empire, the buildings of the past, great works of literature, but an examination of history shows it is subject to change, that it is replaced by other histories.

Worse is the distance between the idea and the reality. People need an idea of themselves and their goals; but what is achieved and how it is achieved always turn out to be disillusioning. One of Naipaul's new themes is the way an achievement does not in itself embody the emotions that went into it. After each burst of fantasy, energy, work and achievement we return to reality. (This is especially true of the writer.)

By the time Naipaul had published *Biswas* and *The Middle Passage* he had won various literary awards but England itself had not become his home. He felt he did not know what went on among the British, could not write about British society, especially the private lives that took place behind closed doors and drawn curtains. Despite having married an Englishwoman, he felt isolated and cut off, another foreigner. Having used the memories of his youth in Trinidad he needed alternative sources of fiction. His year in India, told in *An Area of Darkness*, might be regarded as similar to a black West Indian's attempted return to origins in Africa. It might seem curious that during 1962, while in Kashmir, he wrote his first English novel, *Mr Stone and the Knights Companion* (1963), but he has often written his fiction in a different country from the one portrayed. Whereas the journalism and travel books depend on first-hand impressions and immediacy, novels require reflection and distance on the experience. Memories become enriched by obsessions, analysis and the place in which they are shaped into fiction.

Mr Stone and the Knights Companion epitomizes well known aspects of English life, especially the dreariness, routine, security and resignation of the poorly paid, somewhat lower middle-class staff in an organization, whether business or government. At the same time it is infused with Indian fatalism and notions of activity as futile illusion, a view which it struggles against, and instead offers an existential alternative of life as intensity and a struggle against annihilation. But in this most British of novels (in subject matter, quiet straight-faced comedy, social placing of characters, witty ironies, snobberies, even taking as its protagonist someone so unheroically respectable as a librarian) there is a West Indian subtext. It is as if Naipaul were imagining Biswas in England, a Biswas who owned a house, had a pension, was very very English, but still found life unsatisfactory and rebelled, started afresh at just the time when he should be enjoying the calmness and security of long years of work in a settled society. This is another portrait of the rebel, this time the insider who suddenly sees the void, experiences a sense of nothingness, turns a corner and feels a wind which changes his life.

The vocabulary Naipaul uses and several significant phrases suggest the influence of Jean-Paul Sartre and, especially, of Albert Camus, although as usual with Naipaul the echoes and parallels are light, passing suggestions of what has touched his imagination. 'It was like an experience of nothingness, an experience of death' (p. 50). Before Mr Stone is touched by the winds of change he is the ultimate anti-existentalist. In a typical Naipaulian inversion Mr Stone, unlike Camus' Meursault, is disturbed by his mother's death (forty-five years ago!):

> His life, since his recovery from that disturbance, he saw as a
> period of protracted calm which, by reference to what had gone

before, he had never ceased to savour in his special way. Life was something to be moved through. Experiences were not to be enjoyed at the actual moment; pleasure in them came only when they had been, as it were, docketed and put away in the file of the past. (p. 15)

Mr Stone branches off from *L'Etranger* in the importance of art and creation. Naipaul compares such a way of experiencing to the relationship of art to the natural world:

It was then that they acquired colour, just as colour came truly to Nature only in a coloured snapshot or painting, which annihilated colourless, distorting space. He was in the habit in odd moments of solitude of writing out neatly tabulated accounts of his career such as might have been submitted to a prospective employer. (p. 15)

Such also would be the relationship of literature to life; literature would be that which has passed or is dying. Art would not be actual experience; it would be careful analysis and colouring of the past. Mr Stone is another of Naipaul's writers, the writing reflecting some failure in his way of experiencing and perceiving. It is this flavourlessness of 'solidity, continuity and flow' (p. 17) that is soon challenged as he becomes aware of a feeling of unhappiness. Mr Stone's views are those that Naipaul has at various time expressed. The direct brutal presentation of fact and experience in modern art is a kind of violence which he rejects. But the life of the careful, meditative artist is isolated, without intensity, a source of crankiness. So the experience which went into the book is distant from the book produced. (The contrast between reportage and fiction, between self and art, comes closest to being solved in *The Enigma of Arrival*.) Mr Stone's situation is figurative of the writer. And there is the need to summon the energy to begin again after each book is finished. Naipaul alludes to T. S. Eliot's 'Waste Land' in suggesting how the first stirrings of renewal are frightening. '*Those who doubt the coming of the Spring*: the words magnified and gave a focus to his uneasiness. They recalled a moment – then, memory and fear quickening, he saw that they recalled several moments, which had multiplied during the last year – of unease, unsettlement' (p. 20).

This is a rather different prose from Naipaul's first four novels. The texture is denser, richer, the mood more reflective and seri-

ous, the tones sombre. It is more appropriate for the age and
complexity of the character and his society; but Naipaul is also
aiming at a more nuanced observation of personality, desire, psychology than in his earlier novels. The comedy and humour similarly deepen and become quieter. Literary allusions are
foregrounded and employed as part of the conflict within the
character. The literary subtext has become part of the text.

Characters are identified by their taste, appearance, furniture,
house. Mr Stone in dress is 'a complete Simpson's man' (p. 48) in
a 'black city overcoat'. He is recognizable as one of the many
minor clerks who have been the subject of English fiction and of
the greyness, stories about small lives, that were an aspect of the
English novel of the 1950s and 1960s. Although he may reflect
Naipaul's own sense of the smallness of his life in London, this is
social comedy about a 'complete' society that Naipaul despaired of
writing about in the West Indies, with its supposed lack of standards. Characters are social types, placed in terms of manners and
appearance; Gwen's early fatness and willingness to give into the
temptations of chocolates foretells her moving in with Whymper.
Whymper's lack of neat appearance, his whims for fashions in
clothing, his absurd posturing about how to tap out a cigarette are
part of the same superficiality that makes him an ideas man who
packages Mr Stone's Knights Companions into a public relations
scheme. He lives off the passion and dreams of others; the free-
wheeling fantasy he employs to find the right packaging is shown
in his love and moral life, bragging about and baying for an ageing
actress, then becoming Gwen's lover. He is morally untidy, yet
someone who knows the ways of the world in terms of his own
career. As in Jane Austen's world, manners are morals.

Except for a few details, there is little specifically of London
about the novel. A librarian who works for a large firm, lives on his
own except for a housekeeper, owns a dingy, war-damaged house,
has a garden which he dislikes, is surrounded by neighbours he
does not know and dislikes, is obsessed with the neighbour's cat,
sounds like a story we have come to associate with the English
provinces after the war, when English writing turned inward from
larger issues and was fascinated by the manners, morals and lives
of the drab rather than the sophisticated and cosmopolitan. Because of his own financial and social condition, as well as his career
as a serious novelist, Naipaul found himself living the life of the
drab in London. In *Mr Stone* he uses a Mr Polly character to

explore the contradictions between the life and work of the writer, the glamour of the art world and the work that has gone into it, as well as the contradictions between his desire for an ordered existence and his desire for a life of intensity and creativity.[21] While it is a novel about British manners and morals, the main themes are philosophical and about the relationship between ideas, the created and the creator.

Within this small, tightly controlled world of the petty, Naipaul has portrayed an existential drama of someone awakening to self-definition. That it comes to someone so old, near retirement – the prospect of retirement sets off the drama – is why we might not realize that Mr Stone is a brother to Camus' rebel, although in the many references to Stone's solitude and loneliness, and in his lack of close relationships, we can see the alienation, the significant toneless voice, of Camus' Outsider.

As with many of Naipaul's later novels the events are few, the narrative imprecise about what actually happens, the story simple and the space filled with details of scenes and conversation rather than actions. Although the narrator is always in control – characters here do not come alive and offer alternative visions, alternative perspectives – there is a polyphony of a kind, of conflicting attitudes, even world views, within the main character and the author. Mr Stone begins by seeing himself as part of the slow, steady continuity of nature. The tree he watches with its seasonal changes is seen by him as symbolic of himself. This is surprising since the seasonal image of change usually suggests sexual renewal, vitality, not a steady decay into old age and retirement. Within the symbol itself there is a contradiction, especially as its use by Mr Stone is the opposite of the expected. But there are early hints of change. Mr Stone has more physical energy than is in keeping with his restricting vision of the world. His garden is a way to work off the energy. Soon the vitality will find expression in a marriage, then in his scheme for a plan to keep retired company employees engaged in visiting each other, then in the developing of the idea into a workable package and programme. Finally he will be left dissatisfied, realizing that his one idea cannot support him emotionally further. Once it is achieved there is nothing new for him to do with it and it has become something that others will administer. Whymper, who deals in ideas, moves on to a better job, whereas Mr Stone has only his retirement and wife to which to look forward.

Mr Stone has learned that such frustration and depression pass; symbolically there is a sign of renewal in his looking forward to seeing the young black cat, whereas at the novel's opening he regarded that black cat as his enemy. Whatever happens to Mr Stone now he will have an interest in life. Even Margaret, his wife, has become part of his world; he no longer feels such isolation and loneliness. The obvious analogy is to a writer who, having completed a novel and passed it on to the publisher and his publicity department, returns to his desk, solitude and family, awaiting the creative pain of starting again!

If in the opening of the novel 'nature' might be seen as a kind of Indian fatalism, a withdrawal from the life of desire, the ending of the novel includes an Indian subtext. The conclusion picks up many motifs from earlier chapters. Mr Stone 'had a vision of the city such as he had once before, at the first dinner party he and Margaret had given' (p. 125; see p. 42 for the parallel). 'He stripped the city of all that was enduring and saw that all that was not flesh was of no importance to man. All that mattered was man's own frailty and corruptibility. The order of the universe, to which he had sought to ally himself, was not his order' (p. 125). This existential view of man alone in an alien, changing, uncaring universe is qualified by: 'but now he saw, too, that it was not by creation that man demonstrated his power and defied this hostile order, but by destruction. By damming the river, by destroying the mountain, by so scarring the face of the earth that Nature's attempt to reassert herself became a mockery' (p. 125). This destruction seen in the houses and gardens of his street might remind us of the three aspects of the divine in Indian philosophy – creation, being, destruction. Mr Stone embodies the creative; 'He was no destroyer' (p. 126). These are the three faces of Shiva as creator, preserver, destroyer.

Mr Stone and the Knights Companion might be seen in relation to *A House for Mr Biswas*. It has many of the same elements. It follows a similar structure of the first half consisting of aimless discontent, the new start at the middle (chapter 4), the return to the motifs of the opening at the conclusion. In the first half of both novels the main character makes a rapid and unsatisfying marriage; in the second half he comes gradually to accept his wife until at the conclusion he depends on her companionship. (This is the Indian model which results from arranged marriages in contrast to Western love marriages.) In both novels the triumphs of the second half are deflated as the main character finds that his own expansion in the outside world is dependent on others, especially institutions, and he is eventually defeated as he no longer is of use to others. At the end of the novel his previous triumphs have made life worthwhile. Biswas retires (for medical reasons) and dies. Stone is awaiting retirement and hopes for renewal.

Many of the same symbols occur in both novels, such as the use of Christmas to mark the passing of the years, and, of course, the significance of the house. Mr Stone is what Biswas' life might have been like in England, and what V. S. Naipaul's life is like as a writer. Security, a homogeneous society, a pension, cultural roots, a home, is an attractive ideal, but the energies of life, the desire for stimulus, the need for change, the need to conquer, to achieve, for what Hobbes termed glorification, even the need for new companionship, create the uprooted rebel, the artist, the modern individual, and put us in the existential situation of self-creation, a self-creation limited however by our circumstances and society. At the end of the novel Mr Stone has returned to a wasteland-like mood, but now he knows it will change; such renewal is part of nature. It is also the condition of the artist's imagination; this is the period of depression before the return of the muse.

In this sober but amusing novel one of the most striking effects is the way Mr Stone's courtship of Margaret (love occupies a large proportion of most European and American novels) is rapidly disposed of at the end of chapter 1 in a single sentence in which sexuality and seasonal renewal are figured in the buds of a tree: 'In the second week of March Mr Stone and Mrs Springer were married when on the tree in the school grounds the buds had swollen and in sunshine were like points of white' (p. 27). Then in chapter 2 Mr Stone (a bit like Biswas) tries to avoid the consequences of being married, pretending it never really happened and nothing much has changed. But at the novel's end he is waiting 'alone' in 'the empty house' (like Biswas) for Margaret.

Mr Stone and the Knights Companion was written in Kashmir in 1962 during a year when Naipaul was examining his relationship to India. At the end of the year Naipaul acknowledged in *An Area of Darkness* (1964) that while he was familiar with Indian customs he remained an outsider, a product of Trinidad and the New World, someone with Western instincts concerning the worth of the individual, social justice, activity, accomplishment, the present. Indian habits of passivity, fatalism and other worldliness, even self-centredness, are attractive and a recognizable part of himself, but he is not part of the society and sees it from outside as someone with Western-educated eyes and values. Looking for signs of a great culture and history from which he has been displaced by the Indian version of the middle passage, he finds instead shrunken bodies, feudal social and economic relations which dehumanize, incompetence, political bluster, general corruption, a lack of concern with others and the continuing importance of ritual and habit at the expense of human relations and efficiency. Worse, he finds Indians unable or unwilling to see their problems and act rationally. The excrement that he often mentions is real and representative of decay. What was once part of personal health has become ritualized into custom and no longer noticed. Instead of building latrines, being concerned with communal health and public appearances, there is the self-centred concern with evacuating impurities regardless of the consequences to society. This assumes the continuation of a caste system in which part of the population is considered subhuman, beneath notice and enslaved to such tasks as sweeping and taking away the excrement of others.

If the excrement and untouchables in *An Area of Darkness* represent a decayed older India which co-exists with the modern state and remains at its core, preventing India from being whatever Naipaul hoped to find, Indian history and monuments prove also to be disillusioning. Typical is the pilgrimage to the Cave of Amarnath, the Eternal Lord, in chapter 7. There is an elaborate and costly preparation, during which Indian petty corruption and untruthfulness are revealed, an exhausting trip, communal hysteria, overcrowding, forced chanting and ritualistic praise of the God, but the massive ice phallus either has not formed or has melted and there is nothing there to see or even to regard as a symbol. Only if you belong to the culture and can accept it totally is the pilgrimage meaningful. Otherwise to an outsider it is a sham, an example of how Indians lose themselves in absurdities and foolish mysteries.[22]

Instead Naipaul's attention shifts to the human, to manners and morals, to relations between people – the usual interests of the Western novel. He considers how Aziz manipulates himself and others for his own advantage. Naipaul's surprisingly sentimental hope that he has Aziz' affection and loyalty replays the conventions of the European travel book about exotic places and the loyalties and disloyalties of servants in order to interrogate such conventions. He tries to see Aziz clearly, yet as with so much of India, he is unable to do so. It remains an area of darkness for him; no matter how much of himself he recognizes in it, he remains an outsider. Another story concerns an American girl and her wild, destructive love affair with an Indian musician. As so often in Naipaul's writing sexual desire and romantic love are destructive. This is another East–West encounter, in which a Westerner is found destroying herself in search of some illusionary India, except that here she has the will and means to escape, whereas love destroys the young Indian musician who has fallen hopelessly in love.

Throughout *An Area of Darkness* there is a sense of humiliation, of a personal frustration that the India of his secret imagination and longings, of his imagined origins, is another oriental third world country despite its size and ancient history. He is angry at the dirt, decay, incompetence, corruption, passivity, the humiliation by the threatening Chinese army, by the way Gandhi has been turned into another saint and his Western rationality ignored. Like many other nationalists, Naipaul wants a modern, Western, efficient industrialized state, and he wants a revitalized native, traditional, authentic culture.[23]

This is a much less analytical book than Naipaul's studies of other societies, more, under its careful construction and organization, a cry of conflict and pain concluding with recognition that the India of his dreams did not exist and what he had lived during the past year was a partial discovery of an India which was both more varied and less ideal. It also brought to an end, for a time, his recurring quest for a home, a land in which he could merge, settle, be. 'It was a journey that ought not to have been made; it had broken my life in two' (p. 265). He returns to London 'trying, in vain, to summon up a positive response to this city where I had lived and worked; facing my own emptiness, my feeling of being physically lost' (p. 266).

It was only now, as my experience of India defined itself more properly against my own homelessness, that I saw how close in the past year I had been to the total Indian negation, how much it had become the basis of thought and feeling. And already, with this awareness, in a world where illusion can only be a concept and not something felt in the bones, it was slipping away from me. (p. 266)

In *An Area of Darkness* Naipaul often uses words like mimic and mimicry to suggest imitation or copying of American or European civilization. This appears similar to the usual nationalist complaint that the elite and bourgeoisie have cut themselves off from local or national traditions supposedly still practised by the people or folk. Naipaul regards sentimentalizing of the past as reactionary, self-defeating, and contrary to the need for modernization; yet the modernization he wants must be different from aping of the West. He wants a will to change, an idea of the self, a purpose, an existential being which is authentic in evolving from the past and the culture. Although his next novel, *The Mimic Men,* is concerned with West Indian mimicry of the British it will question whether the ideal he seeks is possible and whether the solution he seeks for his feelings of alienation is in writing rather than being part of a larger, grander civilization.

5

A Flag on the Island, The Mimic Men and *The Loss of El Dorado*

A Flag on the Island (1967) brings together short fiction written at various times. 'My Aunt Gold Teeth', dated 1954, the earliest of Naipaul's collected writings, is set in the Hindu heartland of rural Trinidad. Its amusing illustration of the way the community was changing through contact with other cultures also reveals the antagonisms at the heart of social relations; such social comedy as deceptions, feelings of guilt and family recriminations results from giving into the temptation of trying the ways of others. An ortho-dox Hindu's wife resorts to Roman Catholic prayers to overcome her barrenness; when her husband, an orthodox pundit, dies her prayers are said to have caused his death and she is cruelly told that she does not deserve to have children to care for her in old age. The aunt's ignorance of the significance of both the Hindu and Catholic rituals she practises, as well as the various ethnic animosities within the community, look forward to the title story 'A Flag on the Island', written (1965) during the time Naipaul was writing *The Mimic Men*. The two stories and the novel are in part about communal antagonisms and the cultural confusions and mimicry of cultural behaviour that occur when different groups are brought together and society is in a period of change. The title story is also concerned about commitment and the dangers of the Americanization of the West Indies.

'A Flag on the Island' contrasts an East Caribbean island before and after independence. The contrast was probably suggested by one of Naipaul's visits home. At first there seems a contrast; where there were rum shops there are now modern American buildings, the wartime American soldiers have been replaced by tourists. But just as it could be said that there is no real difference between an island depending on soldiers and one depending on tourists, so a new mimicry has replaced the old. Formerly Mr Blackwhite, humiliated by English civilization, wanted to prove that black people can write; he imitated English fiction about such nobles as 'Lady Theresa Phillips . . . the most sought-after girl in all the county of Shropshire. Beautiful, an heiress to boot . . .' (p. 160). The irony of 'sought-after girl' and 'to boot' precisely catches the distance between the foreign fantasy and the reality of the writer's own English and world. Later, Mr Blackwhite, representative of the West Indian artist and culture, will reject such novels about lords and ladies, but influenced by the model of African decolonization he will fall into a phoney cultural nationalism. 'What we want is our own language' (p. 182). 'On the board outside Blackwhite's house there appeared this additional line: PATOIS TAUGHT HERE' (p. 183). Next, mimicking black Americans, he writes '*I Hate You*, subtitled *One Man's Search for Identity*' (p. 129) which is purchased by tourists and makes him the favoured West Indian writer of American foundations which lavish money on him, until he wants to write a more realistic novel about a black man falling in love with a black woman, marrying and having black children instead of the stories about a 'black man rescued from a bad white woman' or a 'black woman rescued from a bad white man' (p. 198) that they want for liberal Americans. The narrator, an American, realizes that he cannot act disinterestedly in the society and must leave. The novel Naipaul was writing at this time is also concerned with questions of authenticity, commitment and creativity.

The Mimic Men (1967) consists of the supposed memoirs of a Caribbean Indian politician now exiled in London because of racial strife on his island. As he examines notions of decolonization, freedom, achievement, self-definition and how they are limited by the history and resources of a society, the focus shifts from his original intention to look at the causes of the instability of newly independent nations to his own past and then to awareness that writing the book has itself become a way of life and an achievement. The public mimicry of European forms of government and taste is said to have originated in a private void now transcended through writing.

I say is said to because Naipaul's writing has become more complex, ironic, allusive, symbolic and self-conscious. Works like *The Mystic Masseur* and *A House for Mr Biswas* followed the life of one, then two characters, in chronological sequence; *The Mimic Men* is baroque in structure, fugal in treatment of time, and filled with characters whose lives double, reflect or invert that of the narrator. The discourses on such topics as freedom, politics, self-creation, psychology, writing, autobiography, history, mimicry, race and origins have multiplied to suggest many, often conflicting, significances.

Such a novel cannot be reduced to a statement or position. Everything the reader identifies as Naipaul's ideas, psychology or desires is questioned or presented ironically. The self-questioning irony is figured in the narrator's changing name which, like that of the Mystic Masseur, is transformed and adapted to changing circumstance, becomes fractured and anglicized, as does the narrator. Ranjit Kripalsingh, R. R. K. Singh, Ralph Singh is also a writer, a Singh R. (p. 93) who builds a Crippleville. Because of such irony, complexity and multidimensionality the novel feels full, dense, more lengthy than it is.

The Mimic Men at first appears to be another of Naipaul's pessimistic essays on the difficulties of the colonized in becoming truly independent. Isabella is too small and lacks the economic resources, skills and knowledge to be free of domination by others. It lacks the homogeneity of population, culture and traditions that might provide unity of purpose. Its history of slavery and white domination has resulted in a politics of protest and the symbolic revenging of past wounds rather than the cool, rational appraisal of what needs to and what can be done within the possibilities available. Because the nationalist movement has been driven by racial hurt, nation and race have become confused, and those who do not share in the dominant vision are treated as enemies. While the whites move to safety elsewhere the Asians, especially the Indians, are left as victims of the new black rulers.

The background of such fears would be the racial tensions between Indians and blacks in Trinidad, especially the increasing discrimination felt by Indians under Eric Williams (see Appendix B), and the bloody racial conflict in Guyana. While the violence done to Indians in Isabella is mentioned by Singh ('women and children assaulted, of hackings, of families burnt alive' [p. 241]) the story is not one-sided. Singh feels uncomfortable around blacks and is accused of racial exclusiveness in developing Crippleville (p. 238). His mother even refuses to accept his marriage to a white Englishwoman. The Indian world is racially enclosed, exclusive.

Besides the violence done to Indians there is the prospect of becoming culturally and ethnically extinct, like the Amerindians or like some of the Africanized poor whites, in the black-dominated Caribbean, or the Martinique Indians as described in *The Middle Passage*. The process of losing one's Indianness started with leaving India. That was the original sin, the fall. After that Indian traditions could only either decay into deadening ritual or become diluted, degraded and eventually lost through outside influences and intermarriage with others. While in *An Area of Darkness* Naipaul favourably regards the Caribbean East Indians as revitalized, energetic, a modernizing people, a product of the New World in contrast to the feudalist, passive, fatalist Indians of India, in *The Mimic Men* Ralph Singh is haunted by the notion of the extinction of the Caribbean East Indian.

Singh in school in Isabella, reading and dreaming about India and its history as his lost home, and Singh in London, disappointed at the poverty of his surroundings and the lack of quality of his life, have similarities to what Naipaul tells about himself in *An Area of Darkness*. When younger he was an Indian nationalist (*AOD*, p. 41) 'whose map I committed to memory', but not knowing Hindi, not being religious, finding Indian films tedious, wanting to escape what seemed the narrow asphyxiating enclosed world of Trinidad Indians, he went to London.

> It had become the centre of my world and I worked hard to come to it. And I was lost. London was not the centre of my world. I had been misled . . . I became no more than an inhabitant of a big city, robbed of loyalties, time passing, taking me away from what I was . . . to a smaller world than I had ever known. I became my flat, my desk, my name. (*AOD*, p. 42)

Sandra, Singh's English wife, has a similar experience. Rejecting her family and past, she aspires to fame in London, fails her university examinations and with no hope for the future attaches herself to Singh and finds herself adrift and without purpose on Isabella, where everything and everyone seem third rate to her. She is herself a forerunner to Linda, Bobby and Jane, expatriates in Naipaul's novels who were unsuccessful in their own country.

After the failed attempt to reconnect himself to India and the return to England, Naipaul had become like Singh an uprooted colonial, a permanent homeless exile, wedded to his writing and his desk, seemingly writing about the upheavals and turmoils of the colonial and post-colonial world, but in actuality giving order to his own life through writing. Singh continually refers to disorder and the need to find order. He claims that colonial societies lack the cultural, racial and historical homogeneity, and the resources to satisfy expectations.

The disorder that Singh finds inherent to decolonization has other, deeper roots. As in *Mr Stone* there is an existential vision of an absurd, meaningless universe, a world populated by mankind without any god or purpose. Shipwreck, the Caribbean commonplace found in the works of many West Indian writers, has a metaphysical dimension in *The Mimic Men*. Singh feels abandoned personally, culturally, racially, and by the universe, 'this feeling of abandonment at the end of the empty world' (p. 106). The trees washed up on the beach are images both of shipwreck and of the bleak horror of the cruel universe. The image of shipwreck is one of Naipaul's recurring images and will be taken up again in *The Enigma of Arrival*. Singh's fear of death, reinforced by the drownings he witnesses at the beach, his sense of futility, and his feeling that only what is seen exists (pp. 106–7) and that 'A man was only what he saw of himself in others' (p. 100) are themes familiar from Sartrean existentialist philosophy. Also existentialist is Singh's desire to be part of something larger, his concern with how he appears to others, and his attempt to transcend personal solitude through political action. Such existentialist, Sartrean, themes are introduced early in the novel: 'It was up to me to choose my character' (p. 20); 'We become what we see of ourselves in the eyes of others' (p. 20). He is not certain whether his character has been created by others or whether it is 'one and indivisible'.

In contrast to the intellectual understanding of the need to act to define oneself and give significance to life are Singh's continual withdrawals from decisive action, his failure to do. His confessions of sexual failures are similar to his inability to be part of or to lose himself in someone or some group beyond himself. When he does become involved it is superficial, brought about by the will of others, and he will eventually withdraw into himself or be pushed aside by those with more energy and purpose.

The pattern is clear. Lieni attempts to seduce him and fails. Sandra proposes marriage to him. He does not tell his mother he has married a foreign white woman. Sandra drifts away without Singh trying to prevent it. He watches, but does not help, the fishermen and others at the beach pull in the nets with the drowned bodies. He is seen as a nationalist leader because of what his father did. Browne proposes they start a political journal, form a political party, but he takes command. When the Indians come to Singh for help from violence he refuses to lead them: 'Think about this as something in a book' (p. 241). As a youth Singh had fantasies of being a leader of the Aryan tribes that conquered India and became the dominant castes. This myth of origins is similar to black American and West Indian dreams of being descended from African royalty. But when faced by a situation in which he could actually become an authentic leader of his people Singh withdraws into passivity, generalities, distancing the actual world 'as something in a book'. The failure is analogous to his sexual failures as a student in England and his despair at his life in England. Seeking the ideal, he rejects the actual and is incapacitated from actions that might lead to any self-surrender and involvement. His performances are play-acting. He courts Sandra in front of others at a party, but nothing comes of it and they sleep apart. He practises for a race at school, but once he sees the crowds he will not compete. 'I knew I would never join them, not for that race or the others' (p. 117). The confessional model is Clamence in Albert Camus' *The Fall*, which mixes autobiographical self-examination with a parody of Sartre's criticism of Camus' supposed lack of engagement.

Works of fiction in which the central character is the narrator present a problem in deciding what such characters knowingly reveal about themselves and what is implanted as an irony by the author. In such a layered, richly textured, complexly organized, allusive novel as *The Mimic Men* the problem of conscious self-revelation by Singh or even Naipaul is impossible to untangle, especially as the focus keeps rapidly, subtly shifting from the story to allusions to well known events which occurred in Africa and the Caribbean, generalizations about politics and the world, literary allusions and even suggestions that this is in some way Naipaul's own spiritual and emotional autobiography. A Trinidadian reader should recognize the many allusions to local political events between 1930 and 1960 and to local politicians; the racial riots are from Guyana and Trinidad.

The Mimic Men is a novel about how the personal, including awareness of why one has not chosen the active, worldly life, is transformed into a book. It is in the modernist literary convention of writing a book about the book you are reading. It is a Caribbean

East Indian rewriting of *A Portrait of the Artist* and *Remembrance of things past*. It is also, as in *A Bend in the River*, another novel in which Naipaul blends the writing of history, autobiography and fiction as if he were saying that in our time only the novelist is likely to make sense of the chaos in which we live. Yet at the same time it subverts itself. 'For there is no such thing as history nowadays; there are only manifestos and antiquarian research; and on the subject of empire there is only the pamphleteering of churls' (p. 32). As Naipaul is known to enjoy reading Roman history, this alerts us to possible autobiographical implications, but as signalled by 'churls', the curmudgeonly tone that he often gives Singh in the first part of the novel indicates the author's own sense of ironic awareness and warns us not to be literal minded about personal sources. Singh is one of Naipaul's more unlikable narrators.

The Mimic Men continually alludes to one of its models, and in alluding to it warns the reader not to take it too far as the explanation of the novel. Singh's many echoes of and allusions to T. S. Eliot's poems – especially 'The Love Song of J. Alfred Prufrock', 'The Waste Land', 'The Hollow Men' and 'Gerontion' – comment on and ironize his behaviour. He is self-aware; he, as well as those he criticizes, is a Mimic Man – he is given his character of a West Indian dandy by Lieni. Such allusions imply that like Eliot's poems the significances of the novel are both personal and cultural, while showing an awareness that the discontents and feelings are absurd, literary mimicry; the opinions offered are both a serious analysis of cultural politics and the projection of a personal unhappiness, an unhappiness which may result as much from the solitary task of writing and reading as from experience. The novel is a novel because it avoids the stereotypical simplifications of nationalism and of anti-nationalism. It asks whether most political actions and rhetoric are not disguises for personal wounds.

There is no way to get a firm handle on *The Mimic Men*, no way the novel can be reduced to a meaning or a set of meanings. There are too many discourses, often of a contradictory, mutually cancelling nature, going at once; the work is constructed as a labyrinth which, while seeming to take the reader in one direction and then another, circles around on itself while each step is loaded with ambiguity and ironies. There is an analysis of the problems of the decolonization of the third world; questions whether authentic independence is possible where there is a lack of resources and a mixture of peoples without shared aims and culture; awareness of the endangered position of the Indian diaspora in alien lands where politics are driven by the legacy of black humiliation and where political leadership may have no other politics or foundation than racial assertion and messianic hopes.

The novel is also concerned metaphysically about the lack of purpose in the universe, the need to act to create purpose, the ways in which the illusion of significance may be given by cultural traditions, history, seemingly homogeneous and powerful societies, famous cities. If the novel looks critically at the contemporary fashion for decolonization and nationalist assertion, finding threats of disorder, it also looks critically at myths of order. There is no ideal city, whether Rome, London or the City of God. There are only ideas of such an ideal. The only order is that given to the chaos of individual lives by writing about them, by creating narratives.

The novel questions itself, in the sense of continually undermining the narrator, both through the Eliotic ironies and also in Singh's self-awareness that his own sense of disorder may be psychological, a projection of his own distress, written on to the world wherever he goes. Most of the novel treats of his life, not the life of politics. To read *The Mimic Men* primarily for its politics is to distort its emphasis and what is given space. A father's insecurity and distress is passed on to a son who is shamed by his father's incompetence and abandonment of the family for a futile political gesture. The son attaches himself to a wealthy branch of the family which can provide him with a 'solid', seemingly secure house. But he learns that this security and order is threatened by the unwillingness of the poor to accept authority. The son is also troubled by his Indianness in the New World, both attempting to Anglicize himself and dreaming of an idealized Indian past to which he will return. He also fears the extinction of his racial and cultural self. His fears are linked to a self-defensive pride, a dandyism (not dissimilar to the self-protective irony of Anand in *Biswas*) which is expressed in an unwillingness to compete or fight, attitudes of superiority, concern with how he appears to others, the cultivation of disdain for that which is flawed and imperfect. Such defensiveness makes him withdraw from active life, except when leadership or roles are thrust upon him by others, whether in politics or sex. He retreats into poses of indifference, negativity and an implied Hindu spirituality. If Singh in his Eliotic hollow men postures confesses that 'in that period intensity of emotion was the thing I never achieved' (p. 32), elsewhere he absurdly insists on having freed himself from attachment and having fulfilled the four stages of life prescribed by 'our Aryan ancestors' (pp. 250–1). In an English hotel!

Singh and Naipaul offer the reader various explanations for such hollowness and mimicry beyond fear of being hurt, insecurity and apathy. One theme which is foregrounded is that Singh has never grown up, never emotionally matured. There is his low sexual energy and his repeated desire to return to suckling breasts. This is similar to his dream of a homogeneous, organic traditional life and is parallel to his fear of living in a purposeless, disorderly universe. Another explanation is the fracture brought about by leaving Isabella for England. There are also vague allusions to a distressed mental condition in England.

In *The Mimic Men* Naipaul alludes to and disguises events in his father's life (the mental collapse that led to years of living apart from the family, the father's fear of annihilation which was passed on to the son, the traditional Indian horse ritual which orthodox members of the family forced the father to perform as expiation for challenging them) and to events from his own life (his mental collapse at Oxford, his sense of futility in London, the attraction to withdrawal he felt in India). But perhaps most important are Naipaul's own conflicted feelings about being a writer. He has often spoke of writing as a vocation and as the best means of investigating and making sense of life. He has also complained of its solitary nature, of the long labours without much profit, of the crankiness of writers. Singh is a parody of the writer, someone who thinks writing is easy, but he is also a Naipaul-like figure who has made writing his life and who in writing about the world really is writing about himself and his discontents. As usual Naipaul has been there long before his critics, examining himself, criticizing, even exaggerating his possible faults. Although he correctly has a reputation as a realist, a writer super-accurate in his descriptions, rational and analytical in his treatment of the world, he can be a Nabokov creating multilayered labyrinths filled with private jokes, allusions, paradoxes, parodies, false clues, literary games and possible interpretations. If *The Mimic Men* is in parts about the newly decolonized nations it is also about exiles who claim to be writing about the third world when they are writing about themselves.

The Mimic Men might be regarded as post-modernist, post-colonial. Naipaul has moved beyond the realism of colonial fiction to a manner which in its lack of straightforward narrative and its various convolutions, shifts in time, changes of explanations, sense of defeat and withdrawal, appears to reflect the disorder of the post-colonial world. It is never clear what Singh intends by writing his book, his purpose keeps changing until the act of writing itself becomes his existence, a mimicry of a life, a mimicry of the writer's life. Among the many literary allusions and echoes in the novel, Singh in his hotel basking in approval from his Lord and Lady recalls Gulliver among the Houyhnhnms, Proust in his cork-lined room and V. S. Naipaul seated at a similar desk in his Kashmiri hotel. Gordon Rohlehr has noticed how *The Mimic Men* is an inversion of Ralph Ellison's *The Invisible Man*; except that Naipaul progressively withdraws attributes from his main character and leaves him invisible, an Indian alone in an English hotel room in which he writes the novel. Both books are figurative of the history of a minority, but rather than racial assertion there is withdrawal to the world of books.[24]

Singh's many comments about his active life being parenthetical allude to the structure of the novel which is constructed as a series of parentheses.[25] The first section of the novel consists mostly of memories of Singh's days as a student in London alternating with memories of his return to London as an exile and, in chapters 4 to 6, his marriage to Sandra and return to Isabella. In the second section of the book the story moves further back in time to his childhood and education. In the third section memories of exile alternate with his life as a politician in Isabella. The narrative is purposefully made to seem jumbled, convoluted, parenthetical and circular. Although the novel is as carefully structured as *Biswas*, it is purposefully made to seem disorderly, unchronological, a product of capricious memories over a period of time with various explanations offered and shifts in focus. The appearance of disorder is furthered by the way the alternations of times in sections I and III cut across rather than correspond to chapter divisions, so that changes in the focus of Singh's memories seem arbitrary or associational rather than planned. That there is a planned structure can be seen from the novel's external organization. Sections I and II are seven chapters, section III consists of nine chapters. Section I, chapter 7 and section II, chapter 7 are almost identically the length of one page. In a novel supposedly about politics but in fact about parenthesis it is not surprising that section II, treating of childhood and schooling, is the longest part of the book, although, if the readers believed Singh's announced purpose in writing the book, childhood would be irrelevant to the politics of decolonization. Then there are such structural parallels as beginning and ending the novel in the rented rooms in England, the sexual failures with Lieni and Stella being followed by seeing the women with other men, the respect for landlords, the railroad voyages. The opening and closing allusions to Shylock imply an analogy between the wandering, displaced Aryan and the homeless Jew, both cosmopolitans rejected by the societies in which they attempt to settle.

At the centre of the novel in terms of pagination or length is the desertion of Singh's father who both becomes a leader of the poor and absurdly imitates the behaviour of a Hindu holy man. He combines the politically active with the attraction of Indian withdrawal. Such role-playing foreshadows Singh's political activity and his withdrawal. The psychological, rather than thematic, reason for such centrality can be imagined from 'that was to be our last contact, that afterwards we were both to follow our separate destinies and that mine, for all my unwillingness, was to be linked to his' (p. 124). Naipaul the writer in England?

Two intertwined themes of *The Mimic Men* are the relation of freedom to origins and the conflict between freedom and engagement. Singh attempts to be free, to construct his own identity, but keeps returning to the question of whether he is a product of his racial, colonial, educational and family past. At the centre of the book there are even references to Christopher Columbus as if his voyages were the origins of Singh's problems. Thinking it a disgrace to have come from a past of failures he, foreshadowing his later attachment to England, attaches himself to a successful branch of his family. He is willing to share the past neither of Browne, Sandra nor of the European women he meets. He is haunted by his father's desertion of the family to lead a mass, predominantly black working-class movement. (The movement is similar to the various strikes in the Caribbean during the 1930s in which Indians cooperated with blacks politically for the first time and which led to the appointment of the Moyne Commission and the first steps towards Trinidad's eventual independence.) Singh is wounded by his father's desertion and humiliated by the failure of his movement, which achieves nothing but temporary drama and disorder. But, ironically, because of his father's movement Singh is assumed to be one of the natural founders of the new political party which

will demand Isabella's independence. History repeats itself with
independence leading to disappointed expectations, disorder, violence, and Singh fleeing to England.

While the events in the novel have recognizable historical sources
there is an erasure. What exactly happened after independence in
Isabella that caused Singh to flee? Naipaul has argued against
'documentary' novels as having simplistic, naive politics,[26] but the
vagueness and generality with which Singh passes over the events
and his failure to act on behalf of his people are so striking that it
calls attention to itself and no doubt is meant to be understood as
criticism. But if so of what? The Indian plans to nationalize the
sugar industry, British refusal, the racial riots and collapse of a
multiracial nationalist movement are based on Guyana. But another possible source would be Naipaul's uncle's failure as leader
of the DLP to lead resistance against Eric Williams (see Appendix
A). Considering the way Naipaul's own autobiography is woven
into the novel might not the criticism be applicable to himself? As
an Oxford-educated, Trinidad Indian, already famous for having
made a success as a writer abroad, the son of the well known local
journalist Seepersad Naipaul and the nephew of the leader of the
DLP opposition, V. S. Naipaul no doubt could have become, if he
chose, an important political figure in Trinidad if he had settled
there when he returned in 1956 or 1960. He would, of course,
have had to confront the same PNM violence that made his uncle
and Albert Gomes flee. Instead he withdrew into his vocation as a
writer where the violence and political disorder become fiction.
'Think about this as something in a book.' The Mimic Men is about
a road not taken, about Hollow Men, about those like Clamence
who proclaim freedom but do not act. Such action would have
required passion, commitment and the acceptance of the reality of
blemishes. But if in Sartrean terms such engagement would have
been self-definition through commitment to a larger group it
would also have been a loss of individual freedom, the freedom to
write. And, the novel suggests, it would probably have led to a
repetition of what has happened to other third world leaders.
Naipaul has said that the futile Black Power uprisings repeat
the Uriah Butler riots of 1937 and earlier slave revolts which led
to nothing. 'The creation of true power is a very complex,
slow, painful thing. It depends on a lot of hard work. It depends
on a lot of people quietly practising lots of skills – new skills
undoubtedly.'[27]

The formal centre of the novel is section II, chapter 4. Here Singh, a schoolboy, is offered the friendship of Browne, a Negro, who insists on his racial past and hurt. Browne is his double, his opposite, his friend and eventually his enemy. Both are products of colonialism, ashamed of their families and homes, but with different senses of cultural and racial history. They will together bring the island to independence; Browne being emotionally driven towards it, Singh uncommittedly, and find themselves enemies as only through racial violence can Browne satisfy the unmet expectations of his followers. Singh fears Browne's 'interior life. It was not my past. It was not my personality' (p. 144). This corresponds to the separate social and cultural lives led by the Indians and blacks in Trinidad. But it is also similar to his unwillingness to share in the lives of the women he meets in London. He and Stella even find their sexual satisfaction separately. Both sexual and political involvement require self-violation and mingling. As Browne forces on him an awareness of racial distress Singh urgently wants to withdraw.

> Before it had been part of fantasy, part of the urge to escape shipwreck and to return to lands I had fashioned in my imagination, lands of horsemen, high plains, mountains and snow; . . . Now I felt the need only to get away, to a place unknown, among people whose lives and even language I need never enter. (p. 145)

He begins to think of other places as 'the true, pure world' (p. 146). The chapter ends with 'the disappointment of someone who had been denied the chance of making a fresh start, alone' (p. 153). So at the centre of *The Mimic Men* the main character is concerned about his father's humiliating withdrawal from the family and his own need to escape the emerging racial pressures which are likely to engulf him if he remains on the island. *The Mimic Men* is about more than these two themes, but his father and the racial pressures in Trinidad are major influences on Naipaul's life and writing. The times when he returned to Trinidad were usually periods of heightened political and racial tension, with the black-led dominant PNM party accusing the Indian-dominated DLP of treasonable opposition.

Naipaul is aware that his education in European languages and literatures influences how he writes and sees the world. It shapes his values and the literary forms he uses. At school Naipaul had studied French and Spanish alongside English and Latin. At the centre of *The Mimic Men* (section II, chapter 4) it is at school where Singh learns of the Laurentians, Liège and *'la circulation,* not circulation but *traffic'* (p. 146), instead of his own history and culture. At school the children are prepared to be Mimic Men of the New World. Singh's adolescent fantasies and restlessness are redirected through language and reading to idealized lands and landscapes elsewhere. If the first exile is from the mother's breast and progressively from the father and family (including the possibility of re-establishing wholeness through incest with Sally), the second exile is brought about through education and reading. Singh's lack of wholeness, of identity and authenticity, leads to his posturing, dandyism and flights into exile. No place is home. Everywhere he is shipwrecked, washed up.

Education in mimicry is the start of literary mimicry. When in *An Area of Darkness* Naipaul remarks about Indian defecation 'they defecate on the beaches; they defecate on the hills; they defecate on the river banks; they defecate on the streets' (*AOD*, p. 70) we catch the Churchillian allusion with its comic, ironic parallel to England defending itself against Nazi Germany. In *The Mimic Men* such echoes, parodies and allusions are foregrounded, with the novel itself becoming an act of mimicry, even self-mimicry. Space does not permit a demonstration of the many literary echoes to the works of Charles Dickens, Ralph Ellison and Graham Greene, for example. But it is significant that besides the many allusions to the poetry of T. S. Eliot others are to sixteenth- and seventeenth-century English literature. The great house to which Singh hoped to return in Isabella is modelled upon seventeenth-century poems in praise of the aristocratic great houses with their hierarchical order. Andrew Marvell's 'Upon Appleton House' and Ben Jonson's Penshurst are as much constructions of nostalgia for a supposed past order as is the Horatian dream of retirement to an old cocoa estate (p. 32) in *The Mimic Men.* The modernized classical Roman house Singh has built is an imitation of Inigo Jones' creation of a neo-classical architecture in England from the plans of sixteenth-century Italian architects using classical models. Thus all history from the Greeks through the Romans to Singh's house is mimicry. In Isabella the house is first neglected by Singh and Sandra and then, ironically, becomes the headquarters for a political party.[28] So, paradoxically, it is used and does become a place of power and authority, but as the circumstances are not ideal it is abandoned, the way Singh broke off his relationships with women who showed some imperfection. This novel is a house of mirrors.

Naipaul shows his awareness of being part of a tradition of English literature which praises the order represented by houses; he questions the applicability of such a tradition to the decolonized West Indies, wonders whether his lamentation of the passing of order is similar to and influenced by his reading of T. S. Eliot. There is both recognition of and criticism of influence. As all art is built on convention what else can a writer do but mimic? One mimics, like R. K. Narayan, a classical Hindu vision of withdrawal from desire, but according to Naipaul's comments on the novels of Narayan, what pretends to be ancient piety is an angry response to the modern world.[29] One absurdly longs for an ordered hierarchical ideal society but in fact the vision is the product of an early twentieth-century American poet similarly self-exiled in England, seeking an ideal order in contrast to the United States and the effects of mass education, mass culture and democracy. Eliot, like Singh, carried his discontents to England and projected them on Europe the way Naipaul has on the world. Eliot, like Singh and Naipaul, found England disillusioning, a landscape of a lost supposed order and grandeur. Ironically, many literary works which Singh echoes are the seventeenth-century poets, canonized by Eliot, who asserted an ideal order during a time of social upheaval and revolution. But the echo of Thomas Hobbes, 'The career of the colonial politician is short and ends brutally' (p. 8), recalls both the political chaos of the past and that the authority of an ordered society is itself based on the fear of violence. Life has always been a jungle ruled by the strongest.

Words and phrases such as 'fantasy', 'play-acting', 'secret', 'secret life', 'dreams', 'self-love', as well as Singh's self-analysis suggest ironically that his writing of his past is influenced by psychoanalytical literature, which has provided him with a model.[30] This is another instance of Naipaul laying a trail to a possible interpretation and, by foregrounding it, pulling the rug out from under it. The more Naipaul attempts to write from his experience, and analysis, the more his work is complicated by his reading and models which are reflected in his prose through literary allusions and parallels. The more he aims at literary richness, the more he will insert parallels to previous literature. A novel written in English, the language in which he was educated, will be modelled on the European tradition which he adapts and revises to his own personal situation. How to avoid the mimicry inherent to art? Such self-awareness means that every novel becomes a deconstruction of itself. Whether the models are West Indian, European or Indian the problem remains. From birth onward there is the angry cry of frustration, loss of wholeness, fear, desire, and an increasing aware-ness of having been guided or educated into ways of seeing the world. While Ralph Singh is mocked by Naipaul for his desire to return to a pre-natal wholeness, the desire for such security and unity of being is also understandable. No wonder Naipaul is in-creasingly tempted to abandon fiction for journalism and travel writing with their immediacy. But even in such writing there are always models, influences, continuing obsessions. Each of Naipaul's major works of fiction will increasingly be loaded with conscious literary subtexts; in *In a Free State*, 'Prologue to an Autobiography' and *The Enigma of Arrival* he will explore ways of using the laby-rinth of inter-textuality for a more direct expression of the self's experience.

The Loss of El Dorado is an attempt at a fresh start. Naipaul had been troubled by the contrast between the history of England and the way for him Trinidad began with the arrival of the indentured East Indians to replace the former black slaves. The island seemed to have no former time of grandeur, no romance; even the sugar plantations were recent and no longer had a purpose after Europe had developed a taste for beet sugar. The Amerindians disap-peared, interbred with the black population, leaving a few names, including the name of the town where Naipaul was born. The island's history had disappeared into the void, become extinct. Naipaul hoped to overcome his own alienation from Trinidad by reconnecting the island's present to the past. Just as the nationalist movements of the independence period tried to create a usable past, so Naipaul tried in *The Loss of El Dorado* to fashion a Trinidadian past from historical documents. It might not be a noble past, but it would explain the present, create continuity and show that Trinidad was formerly part of the wider world and not just one of many obscure West Indian islands.

The Loss of El Dorado (1969) examines the early history of Trini-dad after its discovery by Europeans. It is a major book, selective in its use of representative incidents and characters; novelistic in its attention to society, character and detail; epic in historical range and its sense of foretelling of the destiny of a nation; romantic tragedy in the way European dreams of discovering the legendary great land of gold are found to be a foolish illusion over which many nations fought, reputations were destroyed and cruelties committed.

In his 'Prologue' Naipaul explains that 'This book is made up of two forgotten stories' which are representatively central to Trinidadian history. There is the search for El Dorado, a 'Spanish delusion' taken over by Sir Walter Ralegh and others. The second story concerns: 'The British-sponsored attempt, from the newly captured island of Trinidad, to set going a revolution of high principles in the Spanish Empire. There was a complication. Trinidad, the base for revolution, was at the same time being established as a British slave colony' (p. 17). For a time Trinidad held an important place in the European imagination as a land from which to explore for the gold of the Incas; later it was affected by the great revolutionary movements of Europe and the Americas which eventually led to the abolishing of slavery and the collapse of the plantation economy, and which left the island an impoverished provincial backwater of the British Empire. Even during the days when it had a place on the international stage there was a small cast of characters. Underpopulated, with no stable society, far from European centres of power and law, the island's supposed governments were a fiction disguising arbitrary rule, inability to rule, misrule. A few foreign sailors would land, the defending soldiers would flee and Trinidad would have a new ruler, another system of law, another language. Refugees would arrive from another island, French landowners fleeing the revolution in Haiti, South American revolutionaries fleeing some new twist in their leader's personality or ideas. And then there were the conflicts and cruelties between whites, black slaves and free Negroes. *The Loss of El Dorado* is an anti-epic of Empire, of the folly of human ambition and illusions. It shows the attempt of human will to construct a new social and political order which after struggle and expectations of success is found to be tarnished and destroyed by the complexities of life, the limited resources available and the environment – along with human stupidity, pride, weaknesses and bad luck.

The Loss of El Dorado can be seen as part of Naipaul's attempt to merge journalism, reportage, history and fiction into a form appropriate to his own analysis of the colonial world and its aftermath. The two central stories provide a wider panorama of

Trinidadian history than the usual story of slavery, while showing how grand hopes for the colony collapsed into just such a story. The monolithic racial view of the West Indies is shown to be more complex, with European groups fighting a Hobbesian war of the jungle with each other, with good intentions corrupting, with evil people sometimes being good, and with what was once a significant stage of European history becoming an unimportant colony. Behind this scholarly, rational, Western account of the causes and effects of early Trinidadian history there is also a Hindu sense of the futility of human effort in this world of illusion. If for Naipaul, unlike the orthodox Hindu, this world is real and what counts, his preoccupation with failure suggests that another, less Western sensibility is also present.

Naipaul spent several years on the research and writing of *The Loss of El Dorado*. Expecting to be freed from financial anxieties, he sold his house in England and began a search through Trinidad and eventually Canada for a new place to take root. The publisher for whom *The Loss of El Dorado* was intended did not want it; he expected a guide book for tourists! Having depleted his savings, an emotionally depressed, homeless Naipaul returned to England to write *In a Free State*.

6

In a Free State

Three of Naipaul's best works of fiction, *In a Free State, Guerrillas* and *A Bend in the River*, were written in England during ten years when he lived in Wiltshire, interrupted by travels abroad on assignments as a journalist. While offering portraits and analysis of the post-colonial world, their main concerns are the nature of freedom, commitment and authenticity in relation to experience and giving purpose to life. Ideas are questioned by actualities. The focus is usually on individuals, their hopes, desires, fears; lives show the real as opposed to abstract theoretical problems of liberty and human nature. These novels are rich in psychology, in awareness of how insecurity is transformed into violence and tyranny. People are often driven by self-defeating emotions, repeat the same patterns of behaviour. Personal lives illuminate the political. In a world without stability or purpose is there anything more than the law of the jungle, the hunter and the prey?

The main characters in the fiction of this period are mostly outsiders, expatriates or alien minorities – those who have become uprooted from their origins, travellers without a home to which they can return, minorities at the mercy of others, those stranded by the withdrawal of protecting governments, former enemies brought together by the artificial boundaries of the new nations, and those who have come to the capitals of the world without the necessary skills and resources to survive. If in the modern world freedom is dangerous, there are also signs of new empires, new orders – the seemingly innocent Americans confidently travelling abroad, the Chinese travelling in tightly controlled groups. Naipaul examines the Europeans who come to former colonies seeking careers or personal salvation, the dangers to the Indian diaspora caused by the withdrawal of the Empire that led them abroad, the effect of metropolitan sentimental 'third-worldism' on new nations along with the tyrannical governments and civil wars that have resulted from the withdrawal of imperial order. What kind of governments will replace the Empire? The novels revise the literature, history and myths of Empire in the light of present realities. For those raised on such writers as Somerset Maugham or Joseph Conrad, what is the reality of life abroad today?

Naipaul is pessimistic about the disorder created by the collapse of Empire, worried about the reappearance of the Arabs and Islams on the international scene only a century after their expanding empires had been challenged by Europeans in Africa and India. In a world consisting of change, no ideal time or place, in which everything has its cycle of creation, being and decay, all that can be done is to create and leave a mark on history, a record of achievement. Sexual desire, however, often leads people astray from their vocation or best interests. Sexuality in its various forms has become important to Naipaul's writings. He has observed that sexuality dangerously brings together people of different cultures and races; leads to humiliation, financial ruin and burdensome responsibilities, results in incompatible personal relations and is another cause and source of irrationality and violence.

In a Free State (1971) reflects Naipaul's travels through Asia, Africa, Europe and the Americas in the wide variety of places in which the stories are set and the focus on the advantages and dangers to those who travel, become expatriates or who have no home. The variety of places and nations indicates that the state of freedom is universal; it is also universal in that the dangers of freedom exist for most of humankind, whether those in new nations or the outsider in England or America. The settings range from Washington, DC, the new capital of the world; London, the centre of the last universal Empire; Egypt, a former centre of civilization which has decayed into an impoverished third world tourist attraction; and a newly independent East African country in the midst of a civil war as the formerly pacified tribes struggle for dominance under the guise of national political unity. Change and disorder are seen as normal in a world in which danger, alienation, failed ideals, illusions, rapid transformations and the mistreatment of the weak by the strong and cunning are the rules of life. While from a philosophical perspective we are all free, freedom is especially dangerous when individuals are isolated from their own communities, where order has disappeared, or where there are few accepted social and cultural traditions. In such situations people are at the mercy of others, people fight, or a new order is brutally imposed by violence.

This is the most 'existential' period of Naipaul's work and for that reason perhaps the most profound, tragic and richest; yet some of the stories are also comedies of manners.[31] If there is no essence, no settled community, if all great cities and empires are subject to change, if the raising of individual consciousness leads to a heightened sense of isolation and insecurity, why should a person continue to live? If individualism allows Santosh in 'One out of Many' to see his face in the mirror, and distinguish it from the crowd, why should he be willing to live a life of pain and anxiety to feed that face knowing that it is decaying and will die? Unlike Albert Camus, in whose writings Naipaul appears to have recognized a similar vision, there is no attempt to justify living by the intensity of experience and the fulfilment of pleasures. Naipaul's characters, like Santosh, are left in the prison of freedom with responsibility for themselves.

In a Free State explores the nature and illusions of commitment. Naipaul appears critical of the Sartrean strategy of transcending the self in a larger community, in some ideal, whether in inter-racial marriage, commitment to others or identification with third world causes. There is no way you can perform the Sartrean philosophical acrobatic feat of being part of some larger cause while retaining your freedom. In practice this means someone (like Bobby in 'In a Free State', Naipaul in the 'Epilogue' or Jane and Roche in *Guerrillas*) from the first world interfering with the lives of others while expecting to be able to withdraw to safety when the consequences become humiliating or threatening. The white liberal thinks he or she is being helpful but is shown to be exploitive and harmful. It is impossible to transcend the self through larger causes, the appearance of doing so is a luxury of the economically and racially secure who use others to feel a purposefulness they themselves lack or to overcome their failures in their own society.

Naipaul does not try to identify with, explain or understand Africans or African-Americans. They represent another culture, an Other, which he accepts as foreign to himself and which it would be bad faith for him to attempt as a writer. He does not know such societies from the inside. He has, however, closely observed the British abroad and they have become part of his fictional world along with Indians and West Indians. 'In a Free State', the title story at the centre of the book, is a marvellously amusing portrait of how the British push and shove each other through language, and of their sexual 'freedom', showing how blind they can be to continue such petty infighting and snobberies in the dangerous post-colonial world. Such a story revises the Somerset Maugham tale of 'abroad'. The British expatriate, including the sympathizer with third world causes, is seen as second-rate, someone who could not make it at home, and even if supposedly liberal, uncomprehending of the local society and racially prejudiced. But Naipaul is not just a satirist, an observer of manners and morals. There is interest in and compassion for the problems of his characters. Having left their own society they are now adrift, unable to find suitable jobs at home, and face a future of moving from country to country.

'In a Free State' portrays the earliest settlers with compassion, showing their toughness, brutality, illusions, hopes to create a better European life abroad and willingness to stay on when times get tough. They built for the future whereas the new class of post-colonial experts, advisors and liberal sympathizers are parasites, with no genuine commitment. They are on short-contracts and will move on when they can, whereas the older colonialists have become too old to start again.

Naipaul is examining himself through such characters; he is an exile in England, someone who has learned he cannot return to Trinidad or India, someone who had to begin again, after the financial debacle that followed *The Loss of El Dorado*, now fated to live in England and to roam the world seeking material to support himself as a journalist and novelist. Hence the concern in these stories with age. The Tramp in the prologue, Santosh and the West Indian narrator in 'Tell Me Who to Kill' feel too old to start again. The old colonial hotel owner in 'In a Free State' can only wait with his gun to be killed and have his property taken by Africans. Bobby, who is on a short-contract and can send half his money back to England, sentimentalizes Africans whom, because of his position and money, he can exploit sexually. Rather than the progressive he thinks himself, he works for and is part of the new nationalist order which exploits Africa. While he will leave when threatened by the violence of the new disorder, the colonial hotel owner came to Africa to stay, and helped, like the Indians of the diaspora, to build the modern cities and buildings of the continent which the Africans take over at independence.

In a Free State explores such varied contradictions of freedom as the opportunities it offers for greater development of the self, the heightened sense of being unique, and the dangers – psychological, physical, economic, political – that result when there is no longer an order to provide security. Anarchy always is just around the corner, the rule of law quickly becomes the rule of the gun, the mob, the army. When people enter a 'free state', society often reverts to a Hobbesian jungle-like condition in which everyone is at war with everyone else and the strong are free to hunt and attack the weak. Freedom is suspect as people are limited by the society in which they live. Linda's husband in 'In a Free State' goes to Africa to create better radio programmes than he can in England, but soon finds himself, despite a promotion and higher salary, broadcasting government propaganda as the news. Having left England there is no job to which he can return. The impoverished English traveller eventually becomes an international tramp and victim.

In a Free State is Naipaul's attempt to adapt his fiction to reflect his acceptance that he has become a man of the world without a home, whose subject matter and themes will be concerned with the problems and disorders of the post-colonial world. The writing of a sequence of stories and diary extracts set in different countries and mixing autobiography with fiction shows his awareness that in his exile and travels he has become representative of the post-colonial world and of the modern human condition. This requires finding new literary forms or re-examining the basis of English fiction, especially writing about foreign lands.

In the five-part form of *In a Free State*, with its autobiographical prologue and epilogue sandwiching two distinctly different short stories and a novella, there are not the continuities of place, events, sequence and characters found in volumes of linked short stories. The 'free state' is a matter of structure as well as theme. While it is probable that Naipaul was responding to the loosening of fictional form in recent decades, he remains within the realist tradition with its focus on people and society rather than the creative process itself. The text is allowed to speak itself without much authorial intervention, although literary allusions and models have become a rich subtext of echoes counterpointed against the realism of the story. For example, Ralph Ellison's classic black American novel *The Invisible Man* (1952) appears to be a model for and is alluded to in 'One out of Many'. Besides the obvious parallels, echoes and similar themes, there is the comedy of using a

novel about black–white relationships in America as a source of
Asian Indian-black relationships in America. (Ellison's novel is
also possibly an influence on 'Tell Me Who to Kill'.) Naipaul's
prose is increasingly understated, dry and objective on the surface,
its ironies more quiet, the tonal direction and comedy or compassion, although present, less obvious.

The five stories focus on uprooted individuals within situations
where society has become disorganized or 'free' and, like most of
Naipaul's fiction, the narrative easily lends itself to being allego-
rized as representative of the nation, the post-imperial and the
contemporary world. The various possible significances of the title
include an independent nation or condition, something that is
not part of something else (like free oxygen) or (as in the American civil war) without slavery.

Puns in English are considered a debased literary currency,
despite the demonstrated importance of what William Empson
termed *The Structure of Complex Words* in the way authors will use
different significances of a term as contrasting themes within a
text. In Indian poetics, however, puns are regarded as serious and
may generate literary works which exist to explore or develop the
multiple meanings of a concept. In U. R. Anantha Murthy's
Kannada language religious novella, *Samskara: A Rite for a Dead
Man* (1965: English translation 1976), the story is shaped by the
various, contradictory meanings of the Sanskrit word 'Samskara'.[32]
Something similar occurs in *In a Free State* which explores the
various meanings of freedom. There is the freedom of the natural
world which has no divine purpose but which, paradoxically, reveals cycles of creation and decay. If there is no essential good or
evil, no divine purpose, then we are existentially free to give life
what meaning we wish, to pursue, or not pursue, what goals we
wish. But this creates terrifying responsibilities as our freedom is
limited by circumstances, possibilities and fears. Socially to be in a
'free-state' is to be isolated, alienated, not part of a group and
therefore prey for others. Freedom not only creates a crisis of
purpose and responsibility but also brings dangers of insecurity
and ruin. Freedom from moral right and wrong also has its dangers as Bobby learns in attempting to seduce African men. Freedom from established manners produces such absurdities as
Santosh's purchase of a green suit. A free or independent state can
be a chaotic, disordered, violent nation, in the midst of a civil or
tribal wars. Freedom can result in tyranny. The various pieces in *In*

a Free State probe such contradictions, beginning with the threatened situation of the tramp (on a ship between territorial boundaries with only the captain in charge), the financial and emotional insecurity of Santosh and the West Indian narrator in 'Tell Me Who to Kill', a civil war in the independent African state or Naipaul's own exercise of moral choice in protesting against the humiliation of Egyptian children and himself being humiliated by it.

Naipaul is using 'freedom' with the complexity that Anantha Murthy uses 'Samskara' or the way that in *India: A Wounded Civilization* Naipaul discusses *dharma*:

> The difficulty, the contradiction, lies in that very concept of *dharma* . . . *dharma* . . . is a complex word; it can mean the faith, pietas, everything which is felt to be right and religious and sanctioned: Law must serve *dharma* . . . Yet *dharma* as expressed in the Indian social system, is so shot through with injustice and cruelty . . . It can accommodate bonded labour as, once, it accommodated widow-burning. *Dharma* can resist the idea of equity. (p. 132)

In the prologue and epilogue Naipaul travels to Egypt as part of what seems a life of being continually on the move, being in a free state. He is also travelling to a now supposedly free state. He travels among various casualties of freedom, people displaced as a consequence of national independence, the withdrawal of the former imperial order or by the demands of individual ambition. There is an older impoverished Englishman, who travels alone and is immediately seen as weak, a potential victim, prey to be hunted by others for amusement. Naipaul watches with interest but fearing for himself avoids involvement with the weak. In the epilogue Naipaul, for once, intervenes in what he sees as injustice and humiliation; but he soon learns the futility of what he has done and withdraws. The strong continue to dominate the weak. Naipaul also observes a touring Chinese circus which unlike himself travels as a protected, well-led, organized, disciplined group. Naipaul is interested in them. Although they appeal to those hoping to right social and economic injustices, they may represent another international empire, the possible new order to replace the confusing freedom of the West.

Between the two autobiographical episodes there are three stories. At the centre of the book the title story, 'In a Free State', offers another, more wry, contemporary version of *The Heart of Darkness*. Here two Europeans travel in a car across a large African country (Uganda with touches of Kenya and Rwanda), while the government is crushing a secessionist movement. There is a parallel between the political chaos following national independence and moral and psychological chaos of the two whites. If Africa has given them the freedom to follow their sexual desires and other privileges, it is also a place of violence where Europeans are losing their dominance, where they are now often humiliated; the expatriate British white has joined the unprotected, rootless, homeless population of the contemporary world and will need to keep moving.

In a Free State is notable for Naipaul's ability to work within a variety of kinds of English. His control of British tonalities and idioms allows the dialogue between British characters in 'In a Free State' to carry most of the weight and fill the space of a long narrative. Each of the three stories is a display of entering other minds, accommodating to other subjectivities and uses of English. 'One out of Many' is told directly by a former Bombay servant and part of the comedy is the discrepancy between what he says, which is naïve, and what we understand. At first he mistakes American hippies for strange Indians long lost in America. He does not understand the connection between the Indian herb he smokes and why the African-Americans are interested in him. 'Tell Me Who to Kill', in its jagged, fragmented, sentences and narrative is the monologue of an emotionally disturbed, uneducated West Indian immigrant in England. Continual rereading does not explain exactly what has happened in parts of the story. The references to American movies, part of Naipaul's repertoire of symbolism, show how the speaker's thought has been influenced by foreign images. They give him wrong ambitions for his brother, excite him to notions of murder and seep into his descriptions of what he has experienced. This is the first time Naipaul has tried to write about near-insanity from the inside. Typical of Naipaul is the social concern, the linking of the psychological to cultural, social and economic causes.

While *In a Free State* has among its characters a variety of the world's peoples a continuing interest is Indians abroad. Even in 'In a Free State', where there are no Indian characters, we are reminded of the Indian presence in East Africa through the description of the national capital as a city built by whites and Indi-

ans, by allusions to Indian shops and mentions of Indian truck
drivers and lower level supervisors. The ruling elite is African and
Africans head government departments and the army; below them
are the new post-colonial experts, British and American, who continue to profit financially from Africa; on the bottom are the
uneducated African masses who are often uncomprehending of
the jobs they barely perform. Between the white expatriates and
the African masses are the Indians who do the less interesting, less
well-paid modern jobs and keep the country functioning, although
resented by both Africans and whites.

In a Free State is in part a book about the modern Indian diaspora.
The Indian servant who comes to America in 'One out of Many'
becomes an illegal immigrant and, except for some Indians who
exploit him, finds no community except among the African-Americans, who his Hindu culture has taught him are unclean and
inferior. He has become free but in terms of his inner-self trapped
and debased. The story is comic and Naipaul has fun with the
cultural and social incongruities that result in the unlikely case of
one of India's impoverished servants suddenly being given the
opportunity of a life in Washington, DC. If part of the comedy is
the humorous reversal of someone usually considered one of the
earth's downtrodden being less happy as an American wage-earner,
another comedy is the servant's social awareness. In India he
avoids riff-raff, judges others socially and has a sense of status and
security. In America he has more material comforts and money,
but socially, spiritually and emotionally he is uncomfortable; his
life is more restricted; and in terms of his own culture he can be
said to have fallen among a people considered lower than himself.
In America he has become a soul brother to the black Americans.
An allusion to fallen Adam in *Paradise Lost* points to the paradox:
'You will be a free man . . . You will have the whole world before
you' (p. 57).

In 'One out of Many' Naipaul uses the convention of the novel
of manners where the servant given security and status by working
for someone rich or titled becomes a snob, the one person in such
fiction who usually upholds class and other status distinctions. In
having an Indian servant as his central character, Naipaul gets at
the underlying assumptions behind a middle- and upper-class joke.
The working classes are usually happier with the security of job
and position than the financially well off and highly qualified who
have more to gain from mobility and who are therefore more

likely to be 'liberal'. Freedom assumes security. It also assumes a
consensus of values and therefore of culture. Santosh's transfer to
Washington and expectation of a green card through marrying an
African-American may seem like paradise to some in the 'third
world', and his memories of life in Bombay may seem the immigrant's usual idealized nostalgia for a lost home, but his life in
America is impoverished, lonely and filled with anxieties. As Santosh
becomes increasingly more conscious of his freedom and responsible for himself, without the knowledge and qualifications to
make much use of such liberty, his situation begins to seem genu-
inely tragic. Naipaul balances the comedy and tragedy, allowing
his themes to deepen without totally moving out of comedy until
the conclusion:

> *Soul Brother.* I understand the words; but I feel, brother to what
> or to whom? I was once part of the flow, never thinking of myself
> as a presence. Then I looked in the mirror and decided to be
> free. All that my freedom has brought me is the knowledge that
> I have a face and have a body, that I must feed this body and
> clothe this body for a certain number of years. Then it will be
> over. (p. 58)

Santosh mixes Indian fatalism and passivity, of the world as illusion, with the rebel, the Western striving individualist, the self-
willed, in which this life is the only reality. The two opposing views
blend together into a distinctive pessimism, an existential despair.
That Santosh can see no achievement in his remarkable life is part
of the comedy. But another interpretation might be that the Asian
Indian is another *Invisible Man* in the United States, someone
whose own culture is mistakenly assumed to be similar to that of
African-Americans, Africans and black West Indians.

'Tell Me Who to Kill' concerns the ways ambition, education,
illusions and travel fracture family bonds and how personal faults
and lack of self-knowledge can be as destructive as the difficulties
presented by the world. The speaker, an Indian, brought up among
the sugar cane fields of the West Indies, is obsessed with his
younger brother whom he decides will not have the ugly, brutal
life he himself has known. Like an overly affectionate parent he
spoils his brother, who lacks the abilities and will to better himself.
The younger brother blames others for his failures, is lazy, lies and
keeps pretending he needs money for further study. The narrator

borrows money for his brother's trip to and study in England, eventually follows him there, himself finds a job in a factory, and besides paying for his brother, who long ago has stopped enrolling for courses of study, saves up enough to open a small roti shop which he eventually loses along with his savings. While he has admittedly suffered from racial prejudice at the hands of young British toughs, he seems in any event totally unequipped to operate a shop in England. He has no friends, no society, no one to give him advice or help. The only person he trusts is his younger brother, who refuses to have anything to do with the shop. For decades the speaker has shown bad judgement about his brother and an unwillingness to take advice from others who warned him. Too much pride is involved.

There are suggestions that the elder brother's love for the younger is tinged with suppressed homosexual urges. The occasion for the story is the marriage of the younger brother to a white English-woman. The speaker sees this as a final betrayal. While he alludes to the breaking of Hindu customs the story implies that sexual jealousy is also involved in his rage. It is ironic that once the younger brother is no longer subsidized he finds a job and becomes presentable enough to marry an Englishwoman. The elder brother's continuing support may in fact have held back the younger brother from becoming independent. This is also ironic as it is the elder brother who had the puritan virtues of hard work, savings, investment, whereas the younger one appeared a layabout with expensive pretences and no hope in life. But he has been subsidized long enough to have some education, a gift for words, and would be more assimilable than the speaker with his peasant's broken English.

This is a complex tale in presentation, insight, psychology and compassion told in fragmented, broken English, using a jagged polyphonic form for its themes. There is a complexity and ambiguity that defies simplistic interpretations. The speaker's ambitions for his brother are shaped, as is most of his view of life, by the many, especially American, films he watched. He is another Mimic Man, another West Indian whose standards of beauty, style and achievement have been formed by movie-going. Frank keeps trying to make the speaker see his failures as the result of racial prejudice, but the speaker has badly invested in his brother, in his brother's love and in his own business. Freedom includes the freedom to fail. Educating family is a way to lose them. The speaker has already heard stories about that and he foolishly imitates a wealthy relative who had sent his son abroad and is likely to lose him.

The prologue, 'The Tramp at Piraeus', is an episode from one of the journals Naipaul regularly keeps when travelling. Here Naipaul is travelling from Greece to Egypt and the ship (as with many ships in literature) is a microcosm of mankind, a ship of fools, an epitome of how the world works and what drives society. (Katherine Anne Porter's 1966 novel *Ship of Fools* is a well known modern example using this medieval image.) The first paragraph immediately establishes themes and perspective. 'There wasn't enough room for everybody' introduces a feeling of people in competition, of irritability and struggle. There are the understated British tonalities increasingly found in Naipaul's later writings ('I ought to have made other arrangements'), the extreme understatement, the sparing use of comparisons ('like a refugee ship') and the short description of the scene which rapidly establishes atmosphere ('dingy little Greek steamer'). The second paragraph emphasizes the smallness of the space, the limited resources and the role of groups of people in the competition for comforts: 'Many of the chairs in the small smoking-room and a good deal of the floor space had been seized by overnight passengers from Italy.'

Soon we are introduced to the 'casualties of . . . freedom' including Egyptian Greeks who had been expelled from Egypt and 'the tramp', an Englishman who from a distance looks like 'a romantic wanderer of an earlier generation' but who is in reality an impoverished, old man, alone and rightly afraid of the others. He easily takes on a representative quality, representative of the loss of European, especially British, privileges (including wandering freely, securely around the world) after the withdrawal of imperial power, the end of generations of romantic travel as the world once more becomes dangerous for those without protection. He is also in his potential for being a victim typical of those alone, those without wealth, status, a group to protect them. He begins looking for company and brags that he has been travelling for thirty-eight years. 'But what's nationality these days? I think of myself as a citizen of the world' (p. 9). Such reporting of conversation is common to Naipaul's journalism and increasingly to his fiction as is the author's intervention to offer an interpretation: 'He hadn't wanted company; he wanted only the camouflage and protection of company. The tramp knew he was odd.' He is also rather vain, another of Naipaul's pathetic rebels who, lacking the means to be truly free, need to assert themselves against others and thus attract victimization. Naipaul with his sense of self-protection 'feared to be involved with him' (p. 12).

Next we are introduced to a group which consists of Lebanese, Egyptians and Germans, which 'had its own cohesion'. It is unclear exactly what the tramp did (possibly he was seasick or had trouble with his bowels), but soon a Lebanese who shared his cabin threatens to kill the tramp. In this supposedly international world people are still associated with their nationality: 'the man from Beirut', 'the Egyptian student', 'the English pig'. Only Hans, 'the Austrian boy', has a name. The prologue itself is ordered into distinct parts marked by additional space on the page after each part. The first section concludes: 'The tramp knew he was odd.' The second ends 'I feared to be involved with him. Far below, the Greek refugees sat or lay in the sun' (p. 12). Each section is rounded or breaks off, a short story in itself, with a striking phrase or description: 'looking like a man who had been made very angry.' The fourth section opens with the striking abrupt 'I will kill him' (p. 13) and concludes 'he was finished'. The final eight paragraphs of the fourth section begin with 'The'. They gain their cinema-like force from a series of abrupt shots in which the focus shifts back and forth between 'The Egyptian' and 'The Tramp', the latter apparently undisturbed by the former's annoyance at his presence. 'The Egyptian shrieked . . . The Tramp had come in . . . The Egyptian shrieked again . . . The furniture-maker said . . . The Tramp didn't see . . . The fascination of the furniture-maker . . . The Austrian boy . . . The Tramp . . .' (pp. 14–15).

'It was to be like a tiger-hunt, where bait is laid out and the hunter and spectators watch from the security of a platform.' The notion and metaphor of life as hunting has become central to Naipaul's view of the world, where the strong detect weakness and a stray cut off from the herd is a victim, someone to rob, enslave, coerce, play with as a cat plays with a mouse. The theme of the better off being spectators of such a sport is repeated in the 'epilogue' where Naipaul sickens at the rich Italian tourists enjoying themselves throwing food into the sand for the impoverished Egyptian children who are then whipped as they come too close to the tourist restaurant. In the prologue Naipaul is a watcher, the writer as uncommitted observer of the lives of others, someone who regardless of how he feels will not become involved. When in the epilogue he risks commitment, grabs the whip, upbraids the Egyptian whose job it is to use the whip to keep the restaurant free from beggars, he is seen as a foolish foreigner, someone emotionally disturbed, who can do nothing to change the local society, the tourists, the ways of the world.

Naipaul when younger wanted to be a 'sophisticated' writer, a world traveller, like Somerset Maugham, writing about exotic foreign places and the shocking ways of the rich. Such fiction was the product of imperialism. He has become a different writer who travels, often using uncomfortable transport and worrying about his expenses, through the post-colonial world of troubled, economically dependent independent nations, the new 'exotic' places for the West, observing the way those in the third world treat each other and the lives of a new, less protected, poorer class of English overseas. The Tramp, Bobby, Linda, are the descendants of Maugham's characters, the British abroad, and Bobby and Linda in 'In a Free State' have the sexual hunger, the class attitudes of the past, but the world has changed, they are no longer part of an empire, they are no longer superior, no longer free from dangers. People from the newly independent states come into the picture as more than servants, noble savages, bearers, comic native clerks, cannibals or wealthy aristocratic princes. Now the British are part of those hunted and the eccentric vagabond, the sensitive university-educated homosexual, the wife of the second-rate expatriate, the rich Englishwomen seeking excitement and lovers abroad, are threatened by those who are no longer subservient. The old roles have become dangerous as power has changed and order is unstable. The ship in the prologue is an example of this new disorder in which relationships, identity, dignity, depend on what one achieves by one's own means or by the group to which one belongs. No one really governs, the law is the law of the jungle.

The tramp, however, refuses to accept being victimized; he becomes a dangerous trapped tiger and salvages victory and a kind of dignity from the situation. He is humiliated and in danger, but he makes it too dangerous for his hunters to make the kill and they are the ones who suffer most. He is mishandled, brutally thrown to the ground and no one helps him. But then he locks himself into the cabin he shares with his tormentors and threatens to set it ablaze if they try to enter. The hunters back off and have to spend the night sleeping in the dining-room.

The ship docks and the groups and power relations that had

temporarily formed break up. Now the Egyptian officials at the dock are those with power and authority: 'As soon as the officials came aboard the refugees began to push and fight their way towards them. It was a factitious frenzy, the deference of the persecuted to authority' (p. 19). The tramp reappears, and while there is 'no nervousness in his movements . . . his eyes were quick with fear' (p. 20). But no one is now interested in hunting him. The tramp represents the dangers of being in a free state and could be said to show the consequences of rebellion, both its dangers – dangers which will continue in future – and the way cunning, preparation, ruthlessness, enable survival. The events on the ship show how groups form and change, how people use others (the Lebanese and Egyptian use the Austrian Hans, he became their muscle man, he physically attacked the tramp for them), and how people are cruel to each other, just for amusement, even when there is no actual gain involved. Such violence may have repressed sexual sources, be caused by earlier humiliations or be part of an instinct to dominate and prey upon others. Societies repress and organize such violence to communal purposes and are naturally in a state of war with each other. Individuals who find fuller realization of themselves in a state of freedom are potential victims. Naipaul's childhood world of a large extended family in which each person or group shoved, pushed, and in which family rules disguised shifting power relationships remained a model for his view of the world.

7

The Overcrowded Barracoon, 'Michael X' and *Guerrillas*

I write from the deepest sympathy for *all* my characters[33]

The novel, you know, hangs between two sexual scenes. The first explains the second. I was very nervous before I wrote the first one. And I was appalled by the second . . . it's a moralistic book. It has very hard things to say about people who play at serious things, who think they can always escape, run back to their safe world.[34]

Naipaul published a selection of his essays and journalism as *The Overcrowded Barracoon* (1972) which includes, along with some autobiography and comments on India, studies of small, economically unviable, islands caught up in the drama, rhetoric and delusions of independence. Anguilla, a Caribbean island of 6000 population, wants to go it alone, but has not the economic means, is unable to defend itself and is vulnerable to every sweet-talking hustler or crook. If only for its own protection it needs to belong to a larger economic and political body. Mauritius, the Indian Ocean island where 'the dodo forgot how to fly, because it had no enemies' (p. 277), was once uninhabited. Since the seventeenth century there have been various attempts to settle the land, grow sugar cane, import slaves and use indentured Indian immigrants for labour. After malaria was eradicated in the late 1940s there was an explosion in population which keeps growing. Sugar remains the sole export, there is massive unemployment, society is racially divided ('rural labour is Indian; mulattos are civil servants; Negroes are artisans, dockworkers and fishermen; Chinese are in trade'), the country is independent, a 'paradise' to tourists, and 'part of the great human engineering of recent empires, the shifting about of leaderless groups of conquered peoples'. The politicians talk about Black Power, idealize Mao and Castro, complain about colonialism and think of themselves as victims. But nothing is likely to change the fact that it is: 'an agricultural colony, created by empire in an empty land and always meant to be part of something larger, now given a thing called independence and set adrift, an abandoned imperial barracoon, incapable of economic or cultural autonomy' (p. 292).

During 1973 Naipaul wrote 'Michael X and the Black Power Killings in Trinidad' which was republished with a Postscript in *The Return of Eva Perón* (*REP*) (1980). Along with the failed 1970 Black Power Revolution in Trinidad, the background of Naipaul's next novel, *Guerrillas*, is the story of the rise of the 'red' (Trinidadian for a half-white Negro) Michael de Freitas from London pimp, drug pusher and muscleman for racketeers to a hustling Black Power leader, known, according to the changing fashions of protest, as Michael X or Michael Abdul Malik, who insanely murdered his own followers in his commune in Trinidad.[35]

The Trinidad Black Power movement and killings were among the excesses of the 1960s when words often seemed real and fantasies were built on top of other fantasies: an attempted Black Power Revolution in an independent black-governed island and a light-complexioned West Indian hustler increasingly aping, mostly for the entertainment of admiring whites, the slogans and organizational trappings of American Black Power until he believes his own posturing that he is a revolutionary Messiah with the right to kill his followers. The dangers of freedom are complicated by mimicry of new metropolitan cultural fashions and by whites who find moral drama and sexual excitement in supporting supposed third world revolutions.

Guerrillas (1975) brings together many of Naipaul's recurring themes – the inability of small, underdeveloped nations to be truly independent; mimicry; the relationship between whites and blacks in which assertions of black authenticity so often are part of dependency; the ways in which Christianity blending with Black protest turns into an invitation to Black Messianism ('Redemption requires a redeemer; and a redeemer in these circumstances, cannot but end like the Emperor Jones: contemptuous of the people he leads' [*REP*, p. 73]). Black Power outside the United States 'perpetuates the negative, colonial politics of protest. It is . . . a deep corruption: a wish to be granted a dispensation from the pains of development, an almost religious conviction that oppression can be turned into an asset, race into money' [*REP*, p. 73]. Naipaul's analysis of the ways in which claims of victimization perpetuate dependency, self-contempt, irresponsibility and fantasy is part of a larger vision in which success requires hard work, practicality, a rational plan to work within the limitations of circumstances.

Guerrillas takes place on a composite English-speaking Caribbean island resembling Trinidad and Jamaica. The Reggae, gangs, Rastafarians, Bauxite, and racial composition of the island (no Indians are mentioned in the novel) could be Jamaica. The way the killing of a black radical leader by the police turns into a black power uprising and the government begins to crumble until strengthened by foreign support recalls Trinidad's Black Power revolt of 1970. Naipaul has taken details and events from the region to create a representative place and situation in which his characters, themselves representative, act upon each other and find themselves trapped.

The 1970 attempted revolution in Trinidad began with the banning of the Trinidad-born American Black Power leader Stokely Carmichael, which was followed by protest groups and violence at the February Carnival and, later that month, student protest. A black power demonstration in March supposedly of 10,000 people was followed by throwing Molotov cocktail bombs at shops and banks, further demonstrations, the use of tear gas on a crowd, and the police shooting dead Basil Davis, on 6th April. On 9th April Davis' funeral turned into a mass procession. (This is the basis of the police shoot-out with Stephens in *Guerrilla* [pp. 166–7] and Jimmy Ahmed's carrying of the body [p. 177] to create a demonstration which he hopes to turn into a revolutionary movement.) Four days later the Minister of External Affairs resigned (no one in the novel knows if there is still a government), on 21st April a State of Emergency (p. 176) was declared, a curfew imposed, fires were started and a section of the Trinidad Defence Force revolted and tried to join the demonstrators in Port of Spain. They were prevented by the Coast Guard, some American ships showed up and Venezuelan airplanes flew over the island. During May order was restored.[36] Several years later, in 1973, there was a mysterious guerrilla movement in the hills outside Port of Spain, supposedly led by university intellectuals and students imitating Ché and Castro. After a few people had been killed by the guerrillas and the police were believed to have killed some of the guerrillas the movement vanished.

Guerrillas does not treat directly of the political events. They are considered a kind of communal frenzy predictable on a small, politically independent island with a history of racial humiliations and without the means to provide a better life for its populace, who turn to quasi-religious notions of racial deliverance. The basis of these assumptions has already been explored in 'Man-man', *The Mimic Men* and various articles in *The Overcrowded Barracoon*. Except for Jimmy's attempt to become leader of the demonstrations, the events surround the personal dramas of the three main characters, Jimmy, Jane and Roche. Their stories show how personal rebellions are mistaken for revolutionary idealism and how history has determined behaviour. The subjective illuminates the historical drama.

Naipaul is especially critical of liberal whites who want to be involved in third world distress. What really motivates them? Why do they assume that they are welcome to interfere in the affairs of other nations? They are to him the heirs of the colonial whites and expatriates of the literature of Empire; now dissatisfied with their own shrunken societies they carry their emotional needs to the former colonies in search of drama, sexual excitement and access to power. Roche, a white South African ex-revolutionary, wants to be the conscience of his race, but, ineffectual as a revolutionary and a reformer, he assumes that the third world should welcome him, give him a job and something useful to do. Roche seems to be a parasite who has lost whatever convictions he had but who uses his reputation as someone jailed and tortured for his beliefs to obtain money and resources for causes and people in which he disbelieves. The portrait of Roche (the name is a pointer) and his politics are part of Naipaul's examination of white camp followers of third world 'revolution' and follow from the examination of Bobby's liberalism in 'In a Free State'.

As the imperial centre has lost its glamour, Europeans have sought excitement among the decolonized. Rather than coming to a centre of the world's activity by leaving London, Jane has become just another displaced person, an outsider without contacts, activity or society. Uninterested in a career or job, dependent on men to give her purpose, ideas, a place, but financially secure and without the normal pressure to make a place in the world to survive, Jane seeks drama in the third world. Her own society no longer offers those like her an ideal such as imperialism or the mission of Western civilization. That Jane was born in Ottawa, has an insured house in London and that her passport gives her the right to live and work in London makes clear her privileged position (unlike that of Jimmy or other West Indians), a position deriving from the former imperial order, an order which has collapsed in the post-colonial world as shown by the riots on the island and by her murder. The new order is represented by the Americans who fly in, who own the Bauxite company and restore order after the riots.

Gale Benson was the historical source for Jane. Gale, a British divorcee in her late twenties, was a white woman who dressed in African clothes and worshipped Hakim Jamal, the 'Muslim' name of a black American hustler, as God. Gale was one of the commune murdered on Michael X's orders. Naipaul regards Benson as showing 'the great uneducated vanity of the middle-class dropout' (p. 14), and 'those who continue to simplify the world and reduce other men – not only the Negro – to a cause, the people who substitute doctrine for knowledge and irritation for concern, the revolutionaries who visit centres of revolution with return air tickets, the hippies, the people who wish themselves on societies more fragile than their own' (*REP*, p. 74).

Jane's habit of attaching herself to progressives continues a tradition of novels in which socially and financially secure women are attracted to supposed revolutionaries. There is sexual excitement in such a relationship. Jane picks up Roche because she thinks of him as a doer. Defining herself through her man is a common role for a woman. When the men discuss what would be a perfect day, Meredith says such a game would not apply to a woman as she is formed by her relationship with men.

Meredith and others see Jane as one of many wealthy white women who have paid for Jimmy's sexual services by supporting his causes. She is Jane to his Tarzan, the white woman who seeks sexual satisfaction in the violent, primitive man. Meredith asks Jane whether she looked into Jimmy's eyes and understood 'the meaning of hate?' 'I was just quoting from an interview in one of the English papers. An interview by some woman. When she wrote about Jimmy she became all cunt' (p. 140). In 'Michael X and the Black Power Killings in Trinidad' Naipaul reports on an interview by Jill Tweedie with two black Americans, in the *Guardian* of 9th August 1971. One was a female school counsellor who wanted to discuss her work and who disappointed Tweedie by not talking enough about race and black militancy. The other was Hakim Jamal, an American Black Muslim, supposedly a follower of Malcolm

X, who talked about killing, and described himself as 'excruciat-ingly handsome, tantalizingly brown, fiercely articulate'. Tweedie wrote: 'This black man is a handsome man, a brigand with a gold ring in his ear . . . tall and spare and stoned on agro. . . . With a woman the agro comes masked, translated into sexual terms.' Tweedie much preferred Jamal's anger to the school counsellor's comparative passivity (*REP*, pp. 39–40). It was Jamal who brought Gale Benson, the woman who became the model for Jane, to Michael X and he was involved in the plan to kill her.

Both Michael X and his follower, the American black power hustler who called himself Hakim Jamal, were often supported by women who found excitement in their macho image, threat of violence and display of black aggression. Gale Benson claimed she was Jamal's white-woman slave and would beg for him. Many of the motifs concerning Jimmy and white–black relations are transposed borrowings from parts of the Michael X story. When Jimmy fanta-sizes that Jane is a secret agent sent to spy on him, it is because Jamal and Michael X thought that about Gale before killing her.

Jane's masochism adds to her danger and it is implied that other women, such as the English newspaper reporter who interviewed Jimmy, may also find sexual satisfaction in forms of masochism. Jane's discovery of her masochism was awakened by an earlier lover, 'a left-wing journalist' (p. 48) who when she grew cold on him slapped her twice and left her. 'He didn't come back; and then she discovered to her dismay and disgust that she was moist' (p. 48). It is after unsatisfactory love making that she becomes moist ('the stained sheet had patches of damp' [p. 240]). After her first sexual encounter with Jimmy, when he rapidly prematurely ejaculates, she is moist, thinks she is playing with fire and wants to sleep with Roche that night. When Jimmy spits in her mouth and forces her to swallow she says 'that was lovely' (p. 236) and 'Love, love' (p. 237). When Jimmy forcibly sodomizes her Jane screams protests but 'Her body went soft' (p. 238) and although Jimmy insults her by calling her 'rotten meat' and threatens to force himself on her mouth she reacts with uncertainty, 'I'm thinking I have to go back.' 'I think I have to go' (p. 239). Her masochistic passivity is shown by the way she accepts being murdered. There is no sign in the text that she fights for her life.

Novels of the post-colonial world written by those from former colonies are no longer concerned with sympathetic whites acting out their own personal dramas against an exotic backdrop. By

contrast, Jimmy Ahmed, the half-Chinese Negro who plays the part
of black power radical for whites is treated by the novelist with
interested sympathy. He is a victim both of colonialism and of
liberal whites. Jimmy was made into a black power leader in England and used – sexually and for excitement – by whites. In the
Caribbean he is used by Roche to justify his place in liberal causes
and used sexually by Jane. Although Jimmy has always been violent
– he fled a rape charge in England – his attraction to the Janes of
the white world is his potential for violence, the thrill of, as Jane
says, playing with fire.

While Jimmy is predictable in the way that Meredith's game
shows everyone is predictable, and will repeat what they have done
in the past, there is also Jimmy the writer. Jimmy uses writing
almost like pornography as a means of working up and relieving
his troubling but otherwise frustrated feelings. This is an interesting Jimmy, who the more he is found foolish and self-deceiving the
more sympathetic he becomes. And then there is Jimmy the half-
breed, the Chinese Negro who belongs to no group, who learns to
act the part of the black power revolutionary for liberal whites, but
who knows he is not black, is not considered black by the islanders,
and who, as Jane keeps reminding Roche, will be left on his own
after Roche moves on. The irony of the novel is that Jane and
Roche, those supposedly protected by their whiteness, are not
secure. Jane plays with fire too long.

A point made by Naipaul's writings is that Amin, Fanon, Castro,
Mao, Mobutu, Perón and Michael X are not what the counter-
culture, New Leftists and other radical sympathizers have treated
them as in their own rage against Western society. They or their
followers kill; and those killed are often the very peasants, third
world people or idealists the revolution is supposed to represent.
Their Western supporters justify or ignore such evils until they can
no longer do so and then move on, forgetting what has happened.
Roche does not report Jane's murder or the possibility of other
killings at the commune; he covers himself from possible blame by
trying to destroy Jane's passport and other documents.

Jane is symbolic of whiteness, the 'white lady' Bryant calls her,
the dominant otherness that has haunted many blacks since the
days of colonialism and slavery. In the well known mythology of
white–black relations, as seen in Derek Walcott's play *Dream on
Monkey Mountain* (1967), the writing of Frantz Fanon, Richard
Wright, Ralph Ellison or the various black revolutionary autobiog-

raphies of the 1960s, the white woman is the white man's most guarded possession, that which must be possessed, loved, defiled, killed, in the love-hate psychodrama of the black man's relationship to whiteness and his own self-hatred. Jimmy's fantasy of raping and then saving a white woman, of violating her and gaining her love, is an expression of white–black relationships (social, economic, political, cultural, historical) symbolized through sexual relations. In the novel the relationship is expressed in Jimmy's premature ejaculation when Jane is dominant in their first sexual encounter, and his remaining erect after humiliating her by sodomizing her in their second encounter. Although Jimmy appears to become insane, the sodomizing and killing of Jane has its logic and is predictable as psychodrama. Roche even asks Jane if Jimmy had sodomized her. (Naipaul's writings on Argentina, as seen in 'The Return of Eva Perón', note how the insecure try to prove themselves by humiliating women through sodomizing them. The mimicry and incompleteness of the culture which results in Perónism and military rule is expressed sexually in sodomy: 'his conquest of a woman is complete only when he has buggered her' [*REP*, p. 150].)

While the killing of Jane is predictable in terms of the conventions of literature about white–black relations it has its Naipaulian twists. Naipaul is interested in the psychology of homosexuality, especially, as can be seen from Bobby in 'In a Free State', where race is involved; Jimmy's giving Jane to Bryant to kill is a version of such a relationship since Jimmy is 'golden', half-Chinese, and has his own love-hate relationship with blackness, seeing in Bryant that deformed part of himself. Just as Jane and the white female reporter seek sexual satisfaction through the fantasy of violence Jimmy offers as an angry black militant, so Jimmy finds satisfaction in Bryant's blackness, ugliness, aggressiveness and image of violence. Bryant is Jimmy's black. Yet, in a further irony, Bryant is himself insecure and admires Stephens' violence and easy dominance. Stephens is the gangster or leader of the guerrillas (in a further irony it is never clear from the novel whether there really are any guerrillas), who has left Jimmy's commune and whose death sparks off the riots Jimmy unsuccessfully attempts to lead.

Jimmy, we are told, is bound to be unsuccessful since he is Chinese, really an outsider – despite his London reputation – rather than a Negro. It is still another of the novel's many ironies that the man regarded by the British as a black leader is not black and not a leader. Jimmy is another of Naipaul's outsiders who belong to and are protected by no group. He is, like Metty and Ferdinand in *A Bend in the River*, a half-breed, a product of the mixing of races as a result of colonialism. He attempts to attach himself to societies – England, the island's Negroes – but this is a more serious version of Miguel Street play-acting, an assumption of inauthentic identities, a mimicry of the imagined Negro, a culturally fashionable version of Bogart and other fantasies. He is a Trinidadian con-man, similar to those whom Naipaul wrote about in *The Middle Passage*. The islanders have no belief or inter-est in Jimmy's supposed revolution by return to the land (another imported slogan). His revolution is limited to his Mao shirt. His credentials are his reputation in England and his being supported by foreign firms. His black power slogans, rural commune and hippie message of return to the land are as much part of the new colonialism as the American Bauxite company that effectively owns the island.

Sex in this novel is seldom satisfactory. Jane's first husband masturbates while lying alongside her on their honeymoon. Jimmy tells Jane he is not good at making love. Naipaul has said 'most people are terribly inept in sex and passion'.[37] In *Guerrillas* sex is involved with, in the sense of intersecting with and being an expression of, power, fear and dominance. The American busi-nessman, for example, reads hard core pornography, *Easy Lay*. Sex is a commodity, a service within an economy. The white liberal English pay Jimmy for the excitement and sexual services he pro-vides. Jane sleeps with men as long as they offer her a sense of excitement, of being near revolutions, of being near powerful events. She needs the sexual excitement that Jimmy Ahmed's danger offers. She gives Bryant a dollar because he calls her 'white lady' and she fears him. Roche tells Jane that she must not give money to Bryant because once 'you allow them to blackmail you it's hard to have any authority with them' (p. 28). Bryant spends the money on his own fantasy, a film in which a famous black actor overcomes racial prejudices to marry a white woman.

This dollar is symbolic to Jimmy. He imagines himself inviting Jane to a hotel and throwing it back to her in front of everyone. He does in fact invite Jane to the hotel, saying that he wants to return Bryant's dollar, but instead he takes her home to bed. After he has murdered Jane he feels a 'void', perhaps sexual, perhaps a loss of tension in crossing a boundary and removing a symbol of hatred;

this is followed by a strange nightmarish vision arising from his deepest self in which a white whore, remembered from a pornographic photograph seen when young, demands 'Nigger, give me a dollar' (p. 244). He feels 'betrayed, his secret known'. So underneath the contempt for the white women he services, Jimmy Ahmed feels deeply insecure and humiliated by being part black and fears white women for their sexuality which represents power.

Why does Bryant kill Jane? Earlier, after Jane has gone to bed with Jimmy, he calls her a white rat and Jimmy promises to give her to him. Presumably he means he will share her sexually, a well known means of male bonding. Bryant's own sexuality is not clear. He is used homosexually by Jimmy, but he seems passively to accept his use. It is clear that he wants sex with white women, that is his forbidden fruit. After Stephens dies Bryant appears to lose his sanity and wants to kill Jimmy. Jimmy leads Jane to see Bryant, claiming 'he has something for you', 'Bryant and I are not friends now, Jane. You'll help to make us friends' (p. 240), and when he sees Bryant with a cutlass in his hand he locks his right arm around Jane's neck and says 'Kill the rat!' and as Bryant 'faltered' he urges 'Your rat, Bryant! Your rat!' (p. 242). After Bryant strikes, the narrator comments 'The first cut; the rest would follow' (p. 243). So killing Jane seems to be Jimmy's idea of how to bind Bryant to himself and is an intensification of the aggression against Jane which would have been involved in sharing her with Bryant. They now share her in murder.

Jimmy's sadism is a cover for insecurity and hatred of women as shown by sodomizing Jane. Naipaul assumes a hatred by the black revolutionary of his white female patrons. (The black radical autobiographies of the 1960s with their ideological defence of raping white women, and Fanon's works would be source enough for this. Jimmy has read Fanon.) There is also the assumption that homosexuals or bisexual men secretly hate women. Jimmy and the other islanders feel contempt for Jane once she becomes sexually available. In his diary novel Jimmy says that Clarissa (the Jane surrogate) will never be able to walk freely at night without fear now that her reputation is known. Jimmy hates Jane as 'a dirty cunt' (p. 241). Jimmy does not merely use Jane as a shield against Bryant's insane aggression; when Bryant absurdly cries out 'Help me, Jimmy!' Jimmy tightens his grip on Jane.

Her death does not satisfy Bryant and Jimmy; having tasted the power to kill they want to continue. When Mannie returns, Bryant wants to 'take him out' (p. 245). After Roche arrives 'Bryant will take you out . . . Mannie too' (p. 248) but Roche, suspecting what has happened, claims that everyone at the office knows he has come to see Jimmy. At the end of the novel when Jimmy telephones Roche to demand that he come to see him, the call may be merely a ruse, as Jimmy by now knows that Roche is aware of what has happened, but Bryant may have turned into a mad killer, threatening Jimmy.

There is an analogy between the South African torturing of Roche and the killing of Jane. Roche told Jane:

> You only have to start. It's the first kick in the groin that matters. It takes a lot to do that. After that you can do anything. You can find yourself kicking a man in the groin until he bleeds. Then you find you've stopped tormenting. You've destroyed a human being. You can't put him together again, all you can do is throw the bleeding meat out of the window. At that stage it's so easy. (p. 221)

Once the order and restraint of civilization are broken life becomes violent.

Many situations and themes echo, mirror or are inversions of each other. Jimmy, after being admired for a time by progressives as a black militant, flees England, where he is an alien, because he is charged with rape. Roche, also an alien, is admired by the Left for a time as a hero of South African resistance but flees England when threatened by a South African agent. In fact neither was a serious revolutionary with an ideology or plan. Both Jimmy and Roche attract women through their reputations as activists. Both go to the island where they are involved in a sham commune in which neither believes. They share Jane. Neither is at home on the island, Roche because he is a foreign white, Jimmy because he is part Chinese and seen as a product of England. Both employ London ideas about how to rescue blacks.

Complexity, irony and ambiguity are created by such doubling or mirroring. Harry's wife leaves him, Jane is planning to leave Roche, Harry will leave for Canada, Roche presumably will return to London, none of Jane's decisions are the right ones, Roche moves on from South Africa to England to the island to England without a plan, making one bad decision after another. He flees England after the South African threatens him, he will flee the

island after being threatened by Jimmy. Meredith's harsh questioning of Roche on the radio is paralleled by Jimmy's harsh,
judgemental tone before he helps Bryant kill Jane. Jimmy tried to
lead the rioters, Meredith tried to lead the rioters. Roche wrote an
autobiographical book, Jimmy tries to write a book which is a
thinly disguised mixture of autobiography and fantasy. Such effects complicate, provide ironies through juxtaposition, while suggesting similarities between the characters and their situations.

The complexity is furthered by the split narration and point of
view. Each of the sixteen chapters is focused on one location or
narrative sequence. We move from Ridge to Grange, with occasional digressions such as to the house of Stephens' mother or the
radio studio. This creates a sense of alienation, distance, fragmentation, bubbles of enclosure, lack of contact, lack of a community.
Each character, along with the author, is sceptical of and disen-
chanted with the other characters. Nothing is satisfactory. There is
no love, passion or hopeful illusion. No one seems youthful. As
each person, including Meredith, is analysed by others and analy-
ses them, we become aware of deep flaws in their characters; they
lack judgement, vision, and knowledge. Unlike the usual bourgeois novel – which Naipaul is too often assumed to write but
which he has radically transformed for his own purposes – there is
no character with whom we empathize, no happy or redeeming
ending. If the nineteenth-century British novel fitted a time of
national expansion, imperial grandeur and cultural security,
Naipaul, far more than any post-modern fabulist, has written a
novel for our times, a novel involving the decay of the culture of
the empire, the break up of a unified vision, including the absurdity of liberal notions of racial guilt in an era when the former
underdogs prey upon their former masters along with the still
impoverished of their own society.

Guerrillas has little plot movement or action and at times gives an
impression of immobility, a stasis expressive of the central characters' own lack of decisiveness. People say they must leave the island
before it is too late but they do little but talk or argue among
themselves. There are continual, repetitive car rides from the
Ridge through the city to Jimmy's commune, Thrushcross Grange,
and back; outside the houses in which the characters are usually
shown there is violence and activity. The narrative perspective
keeps shifting so the point of view is seldom stable. Except for
Harry none of the characters appear pleasant or to like each other.

Jane finds Roche ineffectual, cynical and physically unattractive. Whenever she looks at him she notes his teeth and gums, his satyr's smile, hears his critical comments. There is no love, little care and seldom sex between them. Jane and Roche are contemptuous of each other, and gain little from their relationship, yet they are reluctant to break up. Jane immediately knows that coming to the island was a wrong decision, but four months later she is still saying she wants to leave; she waits too long and is killed. Like Gale Benson, whose murder was not suspected because she had so little role in Trinidad that she was not missed after her death, Jane knows few people on the island and does nothing. She shows her contempt of Roche by bragging that Jimmy was her lover, but this consisted of only one brief encounter when she went in town to meet him (thus allowing him to publicize to the island her availability) and followed him to his house on the grange where he prematurely ejaculates as soon as he enters her. Not even a one night stand!

An important chapter occurs at the middle of the book in terms of length, although actually it is chapter 10. We are at a Sunday drinks party at Harry de Tunja's and the novel slows down for a bit, temporarily moves from the intense focus on Jimmy, Jane and Roche. We are reminded that the Aboriginal Indians once used the site, then the seafarers from Europe, and now vacationers and those celebrating religious rites. Even the new world is old, history moves on in 'ever-changing channels' (p. 119). This is the Indian side of Naipaul, the side which sees this world as recurring cycles of repeated actions, whether the rise and fall of peoples or the coming together and breaking up of marriages. The history of Harry's family is a continuing exodus from some place in the Middle East (he seems to be of Jewish descent), to Spain to South America, to the Caribbean island and probably next to Canada. Harry represents those from diaspora minorities who are homeless and always on the run. By contrast there are those who are part of established social relations, such as Mrs Grandlieu, from a family of former slaveowners, who insults the blacks and yet who is accepted in the society in a way that Harry, Roche, Jane and even Jimmy can never be. She is part of the history of the island, understands its nuances, and is part of what the blacks revolt against. Her house is lovely, lasting, a heritage. The chapter moves on to Meredith's game, the point of which is that we cannot imagine another life than that we know and we are doomed to repeat what we have done. Jane will always choose the wrong man, Jimmy will rape and be violent, Roche will run away.

Guerrillas's revisionary relationship to the English literary tradition can be seen in the allusions to novels by Richardson, the Brontës, Hardy, Jean Rhys and others. The allusions are ironic in their implied parallels or for their satiric suggestions; but here, unlike the earlier novels, the literary echoes and allusions seem more free floating, less anchored to a specifically recognizable irony, and the effect is more disturbing. That we should be conscious of the allusions is made clear by the second page of the novel: ' 'T'rush-cross. That's how you pronounce it. It's from *Wuthering heights*. Like "furthering". ' Jane (Eyre) and Roche(ster) have names suggestive of *Jane Eyre*, a novel in which Rochester has an insane West Indian wife in the attic who dies while setting fire to the house, thus enabling Jane and Rochester to marry. *Jane Eyre*, like many nineteenth-century British novels, could be regarded as ignoring the colonial exploitation upon which the wealth of the characters is based. Romantic love, as the boy's mother in *Miguel Street* reminds us, requires financial security and bourgeois freedom. Naipaul's novel inverts the situation. It is Jimmy who has an ex-wife and family in England, who talks of burning down the island, who keeps insane Bryant as a lover and a reminder of what he might himself have been. Jimmy's killing of Jane is ironic in relation to the Brontë novel; even more ironic is Roche's pretence that he and Jane are going away together. In the third world racial and economic dominance and humiliation are foregrounded, romance does not conquer all and there are few happy endings.

Jane Eyre and *Wuthering Heights* run together both in Jimmy's imagination and in the pattern of allusions. Jimmy's bookcase with the Best Books of the World is a recognizable Naipaul joke – all his aspiring writers collect such series of books; but it also shows how Jimmy Ahmed's mind has been formed by his reading. In his novel Jimmy thinks of himself as Heathcliff. The direct application of such an analogy is that Heathcliff is a slum boy who is told that he should not be ashamed of his past; his unknown parents might be foreign royalty. While Jimmy attributes the quotation from *Wuthering Heights* to the wrong character (Catherine rather than Nelly Dean), he projects his fantasies about Jane, and other white women, on situations in the novel. Jimmy's deepest urge, as shown in his diary novel and in the nightmarish vision he has after killing Jane, is to distinguish himself from, and be superior to, the other 'black'

characters. He wants to be accepted by whites as equal and as a
leader or messiah of blacks. But his confusion of details is also
typical of a hustler's way of picking up bits of information from
conversation, miscellaneous sources and partly read books. It is
mimicry of an education. Jimmy often gets his literary facts wrong,
even misquoting the title of a Fanon book. Yet Jimmy (like Michael
X who had a woman called Richardson as the 'Jane' of his manu-
script novel) seems to know a bit about Richardson's place in the
history of the novel as he at one point (typically such fantasies
change characters without any consistency) has the white woman
called Clarissa. There is an inverse analogy between the social,
economic, sexual and power relationships in Richardson's novel
and between the rich white women and the poor black male,
although in Jimmy's fantasy it becomes again reversed and confused; he is one moment the seduced and the next the violator.
This confusion is itself part of the larger pattern of contradictions
in which he sees himself as rapist and rescuer, victim and aggres-
sor, black and non-black.

Jimmy's language is often literary in the worst sense of that term.
His *Communique No. 1 Classified* (itself mimicry of revolutionary
gestures) begins with the Fanonite-Maoist 'All revolutions begin
with the land' and rapidly descends to the comedy of 'In this spirit
we came an intrepid band to virgin forest, it is the life style and
philosophy of Thrushcross Grange' (p. 17). 'Communique', 'Classified', 'intrepid band', 'virgin forest', 'life style' – every word and
phrase is borrowed, a mimicry of wildly diverse attitudes and periods, or what the counter-culture called life styles and philosophies.
In actuality Jimmy's commune has already turned into 'urban
slum' (p. 19).

That Jane was before her death reading Thomas Hardy's *The
Woodlanders* is ironic, but like many of Naipaul's allusions the
possibilities are varied. Besides the simple contrast between Jimmy's
commune and Hardy's England – Jimmy and his band are urban
criminals, not a merry Robin Hood band of endangered country
folk – there is the more profound comparison possible between
those destroyed without fulfilling their hopes and the tragic effect
of change on people. If Jimmy is a victim of colonial history he is,
as shown by his language and writing, also a victim of metropolitan
culture, especially its contemporary fashions. He is another mimic
man produced by the Empire.

The forest, of course, is not virgin; rather it is on the fringes of 'an industrial estate, one of the failed projects of the earliest days of independence' (p. 11). Throughout the novel we are aware that this is a 'wasteland' and its symbols (drought, decay, ruins, urban squalor) and methods (literary allusions, juxtapositions of images, unfavourable contrast to a past that is itself of questionable value) are often those of T. S. Eliot's modern anti-epic. Graham Greene and Evelyn Waugh had already applied Eliot's techniques and vision to the novel. Surprisingly (although perhaps it is obvious once the literary and ritualist sides of the Michael X murders are kept in mind) Naipaul makes use of the religious, mythic side of the Waste Land vision. Here too people are awaiting a messiah and redeemer ('after Israel') and renewal through violence and blood. If Naipaul shows a modern urban wasteland of 'junked vehicles', and post-colonial disillusionment, there is also the contrast to older civilizations: 'Paved areas of concrete and asphalt could be seen; and sometimes there were rows of red-brick pillars, hung with dried-out vines, that suggested antique excavations: the pillars might have supported the floor of a Roman bath' (p. 11). But there never was a great civilization here.

Jean Rhys' *Wide Sargasso Sea* (1966) already offered a West Indian revision of Brontë's *Jane Eyre*. It shares with *Guerrillas* a shifting narrative perspective, the centrality of two unrooted whites in the black West Indies, an analogy between the effects of emancipation and decolonization, and such themes as dominance, sexual humiliation and the role of money in personal relations. It deconstructed the nineteenth-century British novel in showing how through the relationship of Antoinette (the future Mrs Rochester) and her English husband the British used the islands and colonialism for their own economic interests. But even more significant for Naipaul's purpose is that Antoinette is a victim of colonial history. As the child of a part-French, white former slaveowner in Jamaica, she is an outcast rejected as a social and moral inferior by the British, regarded as alien by the white Jamaicans and hated by the now emancipated blacks among whom she was raised. Her position, created and abandoned by imperialism, might be regarded as similar to the Asian Indians in the Eastern Caribbean and is analogous to Jimmy's insecure place both in Trinidad and in England. Roche's name recalls that Antoinette is often called a white cockroach by the freed slaves. Jane is called a white rat. Similarities between the Jean Rhys character and Jane or Jimmy include her always choosing the wrong man (a supposed doer), her masochistic passivity and her autobiographical diary novels. Naipaul has elsewhere commented on the way Jean Rhys anticipated the themes of modern homelessness.[38]

Words are a vision of reality; words and writing reveal their author. Words and the narrative they make are also revelations of character. Language and writing, even more than clothing, manners, physical appearance and other visible signs, are, in a Naipaul novel, visible symbols of an inner emotional and moral reality. Jane is a 'chaos of words and attitudes' (p. 25), Jimmy confuses being a plaything with playboy, misuses the word Haji (p. 12). Many characters in the novel are writers. Roche's autobiography shows his lack of any clear political programme or even a genuine anger; it also shows him, at the suggestion of his publisher, casually misusing analogies to the holocaust. Meredith was a reporter who wrote the kind of story that was expected. When sent to interview Jimmy Ahmed in London he knows that Jimmy is a fake and that the real story should be about the rich white woman who is backing Jimmy, but his job (unlike that of the novelist) is to report the news that people expect. Jimmy is a bad novelist, with no discipline, no care for words or structure, who uses writing to relieve his frustrations in fantasies where he gets his own back on the world. These reveal himself. Such revelations, even in their absurdities, irrationalities and portrayal of a mind filled with clichés, are sympathetic in their humiliations, desires, ambitions, inconsistencies and failures of intelligence. But such writing is of limited value without discipline, labour and thought. Naipaul is concerned with the aesthetics and purpose of the modern novel. In an obituary for his brother, the novelist Shiva Naipaul, V. S. Naipaul has commented on 'a way currently in vogue of writing about degraded and corrupt countries. This is the way of fantasy and extravagance. It dodges all the issues; it is safe. I find the way empty, morally and intellectually.'[39]

Where or who are the Guerrillas of the novel's title? Jimmy is accused by Roche of providing a hide-out for them and it is probably because Jane thinks Jimmy is a Guerrilla leader that she is attracted to him. But the novel offers no evidence for such a view. Jimmy is alone, a fake leader, dependent on Roche who, despite the island's independence, is in fact still another of Jimmy's white 'Massas' (an ironic allusion to Eric Williams' famous speech about 'Massa's Day Done').[40] Stephens could be a guerrilla leader and Fanon imagined such petty criminals turning into revolutionaries, but the novel offers no reason to assume he is more than a gang leader. Roche, who assumes that the commune was a cover for a gang (in which case why did he pretend it was part of the reformation of society?), is perhaps the only character in the novel with any claim to be a guerrilla; he risked his life for political action. But he is found to be a fraud with no clearly thought out objectives or plans. His politics of white guilt are not much better than the white women who pay Jimmy for sexual excitement and services.

The novel shows a society without the long established inner structures that promote stability during change; since it has become independent it totters on the edge of chaos. There is no redeeming movement, no plan, no ideas, just fantasies, whether Jimmy's fraudulent claims of back to the land, the messianic 'after Israel', black consciousness ('Don't Vote, Birth Control is a Plot Against the Negro Race'), or the white liberal's mistaken notions of personal power and redemption through involvement in the third world. Rather than a worldwide revolutionary movement imagined by the Left and Right there are merely leaderless individuals each of whom has his or her own obsessions, or as Jimmy writes (in the novel's opening epigraph he is cited as the author James Ahmed): 'When everybody wants to fight there's nothing to fight for. Everybody wants to fight his own little war, everybody is a guerrilla' (p. 87).

Guerrillas offers a demythification, a look behind the cant and rhetoric of revolution, a sympathetic but critical examination of the people involved, what motivates them, what happens to some of them. It is a novel of social inquiry, the novel as a rational examination of individuals in relation to society. And yet, because such novels have been challenged by the metafictional, and because Naipaul has had to work at transforming such social inquiry into an examination of the less well studied post-colonial world, Naipaul is highly conscious of his aesthetic choices, thus bringing self-referentiality to the novel. Jane and others are at times described as 'unreadable' (p. 14). This reminds us of the interpretive function of the novel. Third world revolutionary movements, like Jane's signs – her clothes, skin colour, cigarette lighter, speech, progressive politics and sexuality – will be read differently on a Caribbean island than in London.

8

'A New King for the Congo' and *A Bend in the River*

I do have a great distrust of *causes*, simply because they *are* causes and they have to simplify, to ignore so much . . . for example in Africa you can get a profound refusal to acknowledge the realities of the situation; people just push aside the real problems as if they had all been settled. As though the whole history of human deficiencies was entirely explained by the interlude of oppression and prejudice, which have now been removed; any remaining criticism being merely recurrence of prejudice and therefore to be dismissed.

When I was in East Africa recently, I was constantly hearing on every side that this was the Decade of Africa, as if Africa were suddenly going to become technically, educationally, culturally advanced, and politically powerful. I was appalled to find that people who possessed a few tiny skills were so convinced that they, simple people, were carrying the seeds of all civilisation, all culture, all literature, all technology. That was rubbish. . . . The idea that all the things which have been presented to Africa have somehow been already assimilated and appropriated by Africa, is the most hideous type of conning. It may be a willing conning, voluntary on both sides, but it remains conning.[41]

Naipaul, who had spent a large part of 1965–6 in East Africa and Zaire, returned to East Africa in 1971 and Zaire in 1975. His report on 'A New King for the Congo: Mobutu and the Nihilism of Africa' (1975) was republished in the collection of essays *The Return of Eva Perón* (1980) along with 'Conrad's Darkness', the latter a slightly revised version of an essay written in July 1974. The novel *A Bend in the River* (1979) was followed by a limited edition of *A Congo*

116

Diary (1980). At a conference on Indians in the Caribbean, Naipaul said, 'You'll find in the Congo all the nice ideas of Fanon ridiculously caricatured by the present ruler . . . Mobutu says . . . that he doesn't have a borrowed soul any longer; his particular black thing is "authenticity". Authenticity . . . is rejection of the strange, the difficult, the taxing; it is despair.'[42]

Many details from 'A New King for the Congo' are in *A Bend in the River* which is set in a newly independent Francophonic central African state resembling Zaire, governed by a dictatorial former army officer, the Big Man. Like Mobutu, the Big Man has brought a kind of peace – always threatened by violently destructive insurrections – and claims to offer an African Socialism combining the black nationalist demand for cultural authenticity with the taking over of property belonging to such powerless foreigners as Indians, Greeks and Syrians. Both Mobutu and the Big Man carry an impressive staff, carved with a symbolic fetish, representative of the power of an African chief, have their thoughts collected in a little Maoist green book which is sold to the general populace, and have a national youth brigade which marches shouting slogans. Colonial mimicry of Europe now includes mimicry of Maoist China. Mobutu's international conference centre, Nsele, with its model farm and polytechnical college, is the basis of The New Domain in Naipaul's novel. The European-designed capital, like Kinshasa, is connected to a former European trading post, now a town (Stanleyville, Kisangai), 1000 miles north by steamship on an immensely long river (the Congo, now the Zaire). The novel covers a decade from, roughly, 1965, to Naipaul's 1975 visit. Mobutu's nationalization of foreign business took place in November 1973, the new radicalization at the end of the novel occurred a year later. Various events mentioned in the novel, the slaughter of Arabs, the killing of the tall warriors by the tribes they formerly ruled, occurred in East Africa after 1960.

While the setting and portrayal of a radically unstable society in *A Bend on the River* is based on Naipaul's observation of Zaire and East Africa, many episodes in the novel are suggested by previous writing about Africa, especially what Naipaul has termed the Literature of Imperialism where Africa is a backdrop for the crisis of some European or American character. In Naipaul's novel the central characters are not protected by imperial power and their lives are endangered by the rapid changes and instabilities of post-colonial Africa. Like the new nations they struggle for their independence and individuality and they are often defeated by their own limitations, bad choices, illusions; their lives are partly determined by their circumstances and the society in which they exist. Although Naipaul does not attempt to create black African characters in depth – Salim says he does not know what is going on in the mind of Ferdinand and has no acquaintance with village life – the Africa of corruption, a new insecure bourgeois, tribal conflict, food shortages and tyrannical governments is present. The notation of Africa in *A Bend in the River* is not dissimilar from that found in the disillusioned post-colonial novels of Achebe, Armah, Ngugi wa Thiong'o, Soyinka and others. Unlike the African novelists, however, Naipaul does not have a similar commitment to Africa and is sceptical of its future. His deepest sympathies are with the Indians threatened by African nationalism and political disorder. But such disorder is found to be universal, partly the result of the withdrawal of the older imperial order, partly a continuing process throughout history. Is the instability really African if all history consists of change, of peoples struggling against peoples, tribes against tribes, individuals against individuals? Salim learns from reading an encyclopaedia that the universe may be nothing more than fragments of some original Big Bang that created it. This then is Naipaul's big bang novel although the immediate focus is on the big bang of contemporary post-colonial Africa that has resulted from the collapse of imperial order. Tyranny is the probable consequence as the new rulers attempt to impose order on nation-states in which tribal and traditional village life still is the norm and in which the old animosities of tribes, and the cultural and economic insecurities of the new elite, are likely to lead to violent conflict. The modern state, like the technology and the Big Man's ideas, his -ism, is imported, a mimicry.

The political and social disorder is reflected in the novel with its short, episodic, hurried movement. Nothing feels settled, nothing complete, final, reflected upon. Stories are taken up and dropped, characters die early or disappear, homes and businesses change hands, motivation is not fully developed or explained, everything is in movement. People keep coming, going and disappearing. Father Huismans (representative of those with a humanistic, larger, optimistic view of African history and traditional culture) looks down on the other foreigners; but he is killed and beheaded on a trip and no one knows who killed him or why. Salim comments that the Father's idea of civilization was his 'vanity' and he 'paid for it' (p. 87). Salim suddenly returns to using prostitutes; Yvette – the only woman about whom he was passionate – betrays him, he becomes engaged to the daughter of an older Indian friend in London. There are possible explanations, but the significance is not clear and the facts are open to multiple interpretations. Naipaul is aiming for complexity, ambiguity, and richness of text. Even the narration is a problem as there is no clear explanation, such as in *The Mimic Men,* of how the novel has come into being. Salim, like one of Conrad's narrators, appears to be speaking it but to whom and where?

A Bend in the River brings together such concerns as the dangers to those – especially the Indian diaspora – made homeless in former colonies by the withdrawal of the imperial order and the resulting threat of chaos; the need for ruthlessness to survive; the dangers of involvement – especially through romantic love and interbreeding; the universality of suffering; the effect of modern transportation in bringing into close contact such former enemies as various African tribes and the British and Arabs; the threat of the modern African state to the traditional ways of Africa. It is perhaps Naipaul's most pessimistic novel, filled with a sense of apocalypse, of the futility and vanity of life, of an impending worldwide disaster and coming of a new dark age – it is suggested there is a parallel between the decline of the West and the invasion and fall of the Roman Empire. Yet it is also a strong statement about the need to struggle to survive and to be lucid and rational. Sentiments, whether of the past, race, religion, place, home, family or others, are dangerous. It is a book in which the small lives of individuals in an obscure part of Africa become a metaphor for the modern condition of living in a free state.

It is necessary to act on the realities of changing situations, not on illusions. Raymond and Yvette at the Domain are first seen at a party, that nineteenth-century symbol of social order, as glamorous, but soon Salim sees their house by daylight at a luncheon as unimpressive and with its former sophistication manufactured for the party. Raymond, a locally famous historian and the Big Man's advisor, in reality has been exiled from the centre of power and is struggling to keep his job and house. His fame as an historian is already overtaken by a new generation of experts, while research about Africa is no longer of international interest; Raymond's publications turn out to be few and of questionable value. A former schoolteacher who was, by the rapid change of recent

African history, for a time brought close to those in power as an advisor, he is no longer needed and is trapped in Africa without the means to escape to a job abroad. Yvette, his young wife, has lost interest in him as he loses his glamour and she goes from affair to affair seeking someone to whom she can once again attach herself and find purpose in her life. Raymond and Yvette are like Jane and Roche, second-rate Europeans who for a time find excitement and the possibility of being near power in the third world. Yvette is one of Naipaul's European women, like Jane and Linda, who follow a man to the third world expecting to find excitement and a better life but who are disappointed and, lacking talent, unable to escape. Yvette fades out of the novel, her whereabouts unknown as the house she and Raymond inhabited is given to an African (like Salim's business).

In one of the many parallels which give the novel its larger, universal, dimensions, we hear of a party Indar attended in New York in which a famous journalist, advisor to a statesman, lost the affection of his young wife to a younger lover. Love, like politics and careers, is always in a state of change. But apparently not all such experiences are disillusioning. Kareisha, Salim's new fiancée, had a 'romance' in London, which left her with an affection for men. That is all we are told. Perhaps this is another Salim illusion, part of his dream of a new life in London. Why did the romance come to an end?

Indar makes a magnificent speech towards the centre of the novel (in Part II.9) about the need for self-creation and trampling on the past; but he is soon stymied by the unpredictability of the local airlines and is forced to leave the African town for the capital in uncomfortable, humiliating circumstances (a foreshadowing of Salim's own departure) on the steamer and when we hear of him again he has, like King Lear and Mr Biswas, through an inflated notion of self-importance, become crushed, dispossessed, dreaming of a lost past, a lost home to which he can never return. In a further irony it is Salim who now takes up Indar's credo of trampling on the past and self-creating oneself. But his attempts to become economically independent so that he can leave Africa soon lead to imprisonment and his becoming the victim of the African police.

Salim might be regarded as a Camusian rebel, an alienated outsider who, unwilling to accept fate, attempts to live fully, His rebellion begins with consciousness of the weakness and unprotectedness of the Asians of Africa in the face of the struggles for power which will follow the withdrawal of the imperial order. Ironically, however, like Naipaul's early years in London, his life in Central Africa is even more narrow and endangered than the small, restricted society he has fled; his only contacts are with a few other aliens, Indians living enclosed, self-centred lives of their own, cut off from the African world which surrounds them. He is friends with an Indian couple who, having made a love match across caste lines, fear family retaliation and live only for themselves, obsessed with the romance of their marriage and the woman's beauty.

Zabeth, an African trader from one of the villages along the river, wants her son Ferdinand to become educated and part of the modern African state. Ferdinand, whose father is from another tribe, represents the new African elite upon which the resources of the state are lavished to provide a Western higher education enabling them to assume upper-level positions in the bureaucracy. But without the secure community life of the bush, and because of his tribally mixed parentage, Ferdinand is at the mercy of the new political order as well as being confused by notions of authenticity no longer valid for himself.

Although the story is told by Salim about his life, the novel keeps shifting to the lives of others, through dialogue, conversations, long speeches (understood to be pieced together from various times), and reports about others. After the massacres of Arabs in East Africa, Salim is joined by Ali, soon called Metty for *Metis,* one of the slaves attached to his family. This reminds us that English colonialism interrupted Arab expansion into Africa, that slavery was nothing new to Africa or the Arab world, and that Africa has a long history of contacts with the outside world. The novel feels fully populated and is filled with detail and historical background.

Salim is not likable and seems too knowing, too educated for the narrator, although we are told that he reads widely, especially in encyclopaedias. Naipaul wants to combine an Indian, representative of those who came to work in Africa during this century, with the long established Arabs of East Africa. Salim is an East African Muslim who is from a family which has come from northern India in the distant past and who identifies with Indian culture and peoples although, like the Arabs, having family slaves from the past. As India has a thousand years of trade with East Africa such a combination is possible but rare.

A Bend in the River is written with consciousness of being in the lineage of literature about Africa, history and imperialism. Salim says:

> All that I know of our history and the history of the Indian Ocean I have got from books written by Europeans. If I say that our Arabs in their time were great adventurers and writers . . . if I say these things it is because I have got them from European books. They formed no part of our knowledge or pride. Without Europeans, I feel all our past would have been washed away, like the scuff-marks of fishermen on the beach outside our town. (p. 18)

Like many statements in Naipaul's novels this is ambiguous in its politics. It could point to the Eurocentric basis of colonial education, to the failure of non-Europeans to write realistic history or to the way the decolonized learned to become conscious of themselves through Western knowledge – analogous to the way nineteenth-century Indian and African nationalists learned their Indianness or Africanness from European scholarship.

Naipaul is also concerned with the role of writing and the writer to give coherence to, by making a narrative of, life. He sees this as a Western rather than an Islamic trait.[43] Writing preserves and shapes. It is a defence against the waves of chaos, of extinction, the void or nothingness which haunted Seepersad Naipaul and which haunts his son. But it is also a clue or directional pointer as to how this novel is to be read. It creates a space in literature and therefore in history for the East African Asiatics, primarily the Indians, who were driven from Africa in the aftermath of African independence and who have, once more uprooted, sought refuge in such foreign lands as England and Canada. How are they to be seen and to see themselves?

A Bend in the River, which was written in England, is, in part, another meditation on the problems and fate of Naipaul and the Indian diaspora in relation to the rapid social and political changes that have followed decolonization. Those Indians who live by old ways and fail to change are left at the mercy of the African desire to purify the land of others and avenge themselves for the humiliation of the past. Some, such as Ali, a symbolic mulatto, are no longer either Asiatic or a member of any African tribe, but a symbol of those who belong to no group that will protect them.

Naipaul's imagination displaces his concern with the Indian diaspora through various characters. Indar in London is told by the Indian High Commission that his group has enjoyed the benefits of working in Africa and now must accept its fate from the natives of Africa (a situation similar to the Indian response to Trinidadian Indians who wanted to return to India and to the view of the Indian government that the Indians who were expelled by East African governments were the responsibility of the British and not of India).

A Bend in the River is perhaps the last modernist epic, using Africa as a symbolic wasteland for the collapse of a universal European order. The many echoes of European classics are not only a form of metaphor or analogy, they are part of a cultural order, a way of seeing which Naipaul at times admires in contrast to the rhetoric and politics of many in the third world and their admirers abroad. Pliny's *Semper Aliquid Novi*, the lycée's motto (a reference to Pliny's *Natural History* 8.16) is a common Greek saying claiming that something new always comes from Africa.[44] The meaning, however, is not that Africa changes but that there is always something happening in Africa which is a topic of conversation. The consequences of decolonization and African independence may make this week's newspaper headlines but Africa has always been there, in contact with other peoples and the scene of other empires. A quotation from Virgil reminds us that Africa has long been part of European consciousness, part of some imperialism and the literature of imperialism. From the opening sentences of the novel, with its anti-evolutionary 'The World is what it is', to the concluding scene of the passenger barge adrift, there is a vision of history as cyclical, of pointless repetitions, of empire being replaced by empire, of the strong conquering the weak and then themselves becoming weak and conquered by fresh blood, of a world of experience and suffering without purpose. The historical vision of meaningless change and decay rather than actual newness and improvement is made specific in the symbolism of the water hyacinths, the new thing which has appeared on the river and which could eventually bring transportation on the river to a halt, returning the villages to their former isolation.

The Virgilian allusion is to *Aeneid* (IV.122) where Venus says Jupiter would not approve of the mingling of races if Aeneas married Dido. Salim says that it was tempting fate for the town's European colonial settlers to reverse the meaning to approval for the mingling of races. This serves several functions in the novel. Besides putting European and Arab involvement with Africa into a negative perspective, it also casts disapproval on the sexual relationships involving various races, peoples, castes or tribes – Salim and Yvette, Mahesh and Shoba, the Arab men with their African women, and such children of mixed parentage as Metty and Ferdinand, as well as Metty's own marriage to an African. Mixed marriages offer hostages to fortune as the resulting children belong to no protective group, and they lead to becoming an outcaste. Involvement with women of other communities prevents a man from following his own destiny. After marrying an African woman Metty must now stay with her and provide. Salim's involvement with Yvette prevents him from seeing the developing political crisis; he fails to protect himself against the nationalization of his business. In this sense Yvette is a little Eve, her name as symbolic as Metty's. In Naipaul's novels sex tempts people from their own best interests and disorders their lives.

There is a clear linkage between sexual and political fantasies of destruction, dominance, brutality, humiliation. The violence of Salim's attack on Yvette when he discovers she has other lovers is analogous to the destructive rage of the Africans elsewhere in the novel and is not shown in a favourable light. Naipaul makes this clear by its sadistic brutality and by the irony of Salim's self-pity afterwards for the pain he feels in his hand. The scene ends in comedy, with Salim's self-pity and with Yvette masochistically telephoning to console him. Yvette tempts Salim from his goals, but she is, like Jane in *Guerrillas*, an example of female masochism. From *Miguel Street* onwards Naipaul has been examining the causes of masochism and women-beating; one of the major themes of his novels is the way male impotence and insecurity turn into sadistic rage against women. 'The Return of Eva Perón' shows how male insecurity turns into aggression towards women, and the way national impotence is reflected in Perónist politics. What makes Naipaul's scenes of sexual brutality so disturbing is his puritanism. He carefully removes any trace of sensuality, of the pornographic, of fantasy. The reader derives no pleasure from reading of sexual violence in Naipaul's writing.

The parallel to Aeneas' temptation to dereliction of duty also calls upon other associations connected with the Roman epic. Along with Raymond's comments on the writing of Roman history, the allusion suggests a parallel between the former British Empire and its order and the grandeur and order of the Roman Empire. Naipaul's own novel by implication is a modern epic, a twentieth-century epic of the last stages of an historical period. His subject is rather loss of the imperial order than its achievement and celebration. (When Salim criticizes Raymond for using only printed documents and not talking to tradesmen and other living people about recent past history, we remember that Naipaul's own journalism and travel books are based on interviews with people during his journeys.) Just as the voyage of Aeneas symbolizes the founding of the Roman order (and in Christian allegorizations the bringing of universal peace to the world so Christ may be born), Salim's journey to central Africa symbolizes the coming reign of disorder, or the mixing of peoples, the fall of imperial order with the Arabs and other formerly colonized peoples invading London. Just as Aeneas is blown off course and tempted by Dido, so Salim travels the wrong direction from where a threatened African East Indian should go and journeys to Central Africa and has a love affair with Yvette instead of going to London and marrying Kareisha, to whom he is promised. His journey has taken him to an African hell.

The conclusion of the novel has analogies to Aeneas' descent into the Underworld, except instead of Anchises' prophecy of the future glory of Rome and universal peace there is a Fanonian apocalyptic vision of violence.

> At first they were going to have people's courts and shoot people in the squares. Now they say they have to do a lot more killing, and everybody will have to dip their hands in the blood. They're going to kill everybody who can read and write, everybody who ever put on a jacket and tie, everybody who put on a *jacket de boy*. They're going to kill all the masters and all the servants. When they're finished nobody will know there was a place like this here. They're going to kill and kill. (p. 284)

As Michael Neill has shown, this is the language of Fanon's revolution.[45] This ritual of destruction, a revolutionary black mass, is based on the movement led by Pierre Mulele, who wanted to kill everyone in Zaire who could read, write or who wore a necktie. It is discussed by Naipaul in 'A New King of the Congo' (*REP*, p. 187). It also, as the title 'Battle' of the novel's fourth book shows, represents an inversion of the Christian historical scheme, since the narrative moves from a 'beginning' to a promised apocalyptic war between, ironically, the forces of Fanonite violence and the Big Man and his African Madonna mother. When Naipaul was at Wesleyan University[46] he told his students that it was absurd to proclaim any total rebellion or complete overthrow of society as men cannot make themselves unlike what they are. Naipaul spoke of Marxists as 'religious fanatics urging people to destroy what little they have for a dream, a fantasy'.

A Bend in the River revises Joseph Conrad's *Heart of Darkness*. Salim's narration is similar to that of a Conradian tale. The places, river, steamer, country, juxtapositions, and many details echo the earlier novel, except that Naipaul's perspective and that of his narrator are different. The journey is from the East African coast to the heart of Africa. Salim's comments on the 'tides' of history are analogous to Conrad's imagining the Roman invaders of England. Naipaul usually transforms characters and details from Conrad's novel in significant ways, dividing them between his characters. Kurtz becomes Father Huismans, the collector of African masks who is killed by the Africans and whose head is 'spiked', an echo of the spiked heads around Kurtz' hut. It is a young American, part of the next wave of imperialism, who ships the masks to the United States. Salim is forced by his need for money to begin trading in ivory and gold. And Salim, like Kurtz, has a fiancée waiting for him in London.

Naipaul's rewriting of the imperial novel rejects the English literary tradition, yet acknowledges a precursor and implies a relationship which modifies that tradition. In recalling the relationship of ancient Greece and Rome, of Indians, Arabs and Belgians to Africa, Naipaul's own vision, in which the bush, forests, rivers and tribal life are the natural Africa as opposed to the cities of the new African state, becomes part of a universal, timeless perspective of the rise and fall of human achievements. That *Bend* was written in Wiltshire where Naipaul was among the ancient Druid and Roman ruins of England contributed to his feeling of history as consisting of repeated cycles of the rise of cultures and empires which will end in decay. One of the themes of the novel is the contradiction between wanting a traditional culture rooted in the village life of the past and wanting a modern Europeanized state, European technology and comforts. This conflict, which is inherent to most nationalist movements, is a theme of Naipaul's writings and he will examine it more fully in the Islamic world of *Among Believers*.

Some Dantean echoes may have come to Naipaul by way of Conrad's *The Heart of Darkness* or the *Aeneid*. (Conrad's novel makes conscious use of both Virgil's epic and Dante's *Inferno*, while Dante's poem is based on Virgil's.) There is probably an ironic allusion to Dante's *La Vita Nuova*, with its celebration of the poet's love for Beatrice, in the many times Salim refers to his 'new life'; the irony would be the physicality of Salim's love of Yvette and perhaps the Big Man's cult of the African madonna. Just as Virgil leads Dante through the inferno, Salim many times refers to others as his guide: Indar is his 'guide' through The New Domain, Nazruddin becomes his 'guide' to food and wine in London, and others guide him through the symbolic hell of Africa. This is especially common towards the conclusion of the novel.

As in Canto Nine of *The Inferno* the worst sin is betrayal, betrayal of host, nation or lord, as that destroys the contract between men and between men and God upon which justice, society and all else is based. It is this contractual idea of society which Naipaul found the basis of Rome and which Dante assumes is, along with love or Christian charity, the basis of divine order. Paradoxically this is connected with Naipaul's Hobbesian view of society in which obedience results from protection. The Big Man's radicalization (comparable to the East African nationalization of foreign, especially Asiatic business) of businesses belonging to foreigners destroys property rights and introduces a further disorder and injustice beyond the simple corruptions and violence earlier in the novel. This is conscious corruption and perversion of truth and order. Africans are given businesses they do not own and the owners become managers and everyone becomes frantic to amass wealth before the coming chaos as the country slides quickly towards another rebellion. After his business is given to Théotime (another symbolic name), for whom he now works, Salim increasingly becomes aware that he is vulnerable, prey for others. As he needs illegally to amass money to escape, Salim stops being able to help Metty: 'I could no longer offer him the simple protection he had asked for – Théotime made that plain during the course of the day. So the old contract between Metty and myself, which was the contract between his family and mine came to an end . . . our special contract was over. He seemed to understand this, and it made him unbalanced' (pp. 273–4).

Metty betrays his host and master by informing on Salim's smuggling and showing the police where Salim keeps the ivory. Salim, arrested and jailed, comments: 'There were many stages in my progress through the building, and I began to look upon Prosper as my guide to this particular hell.' As in hell the inversion of law, justice and order becomes another form of order in which Satan rules. Rather than Satan we have pictures of the Big Man (p. 276). Seeing the President's slogan 'DISCIPLINE AVANT TOUT, I felt damned and mocked by the words. But that was how I was expected to feel' (p. 277).

The description of those being tortured in the prison could easily be a scene from *The Inferno*:

> The instructors were warders with big boots and sticks; the poems were hymns of praise to the President and the African madonna; the people being compelled to repeat the lines were those young men and boys from the villages, many of whom had been trussed up and dumped in the courtyard and were being maltreated in ways I don't want to describe.
>
> These were the dreadful sounds of the early morning. Those poor people had also been trapped and damned by the words on the white jail wall. (p. 278)

While the tortures, common to such regimes as those of Idi Amin and Sekou Touré, have their reality in recent African politics, the final pages of the novel are reminiscent of the last stages of Dante's Hell and even seem an ironic inversion of the final vision of Dante's *Paradise*: 'I heard that an important execution was to take place; that the President himself was going to attend it when he came to town; and that he would listen then to the hymns sung by his enemies. For that visit the town had burst into bright colour' (p. 279). Ferdinand says 'We're all going to hell' (p. 281) but only Salim, like Dante, can escape from his hell.

Another work of imperial literature *A Bend in the River* appears to revise is Graham Greene's Sierra Leonean novel *The Heart of the Matter* (1948) in which the central character, an English police officer named Scobie, is corrupted by the circumstances in which he finds himself in Africa and like Salim slips from honesty into minor crimes, adultery, bribery, betrayal (of his servant Ali, his wife and nation) and eventually damns himself in suicide.[47] Metty's real name is Ali, Metty being a corruption of *metis*. The relationship between Scobie and Helen is analogous to that between Salim and Yvette; Scobie helps smuggle diamonds, Salim smuggles ivory. But whereas the tempter and devil of Greene's novel of a just man's descent into Hell is a Syrian shopkeeper, here the central character is an Indian shopkeeper. Whereas Greene sentimentalizes African corruption as innocent, Naipaul sees it historically as part of the general political and social disorder which results from the mixing of culture and the imposition of a European notion of the state on African tribes. Chinua Achebe also blames the widespread corruption found in Nigeria on the coming together of various cultures and the effect of foreign rule on previously self-contained tribal societies in which the people of the community would prevent any excess of injustice or illegality. If in Naipaul's novels there is at times a view that corruption, moral and political chaos, comes from the mixing of peoples, we might remember that Trinidad was notorious for corruption. Such corruption is not only African. When Nazruddin moves to Canada he is swindled; and when he says that society cannot exist if people do not keep to their word he is told to go back to Africa. But (as shown by the allusions to Dido and the references to slavery and illegal trade in the past) there are suggestions that Africa has a long history of moral temptation. These notions also exist alongside a vision of all history and all cultures being no more than the conquest and exploitation of the weak by the strong, the slow by the cunning.

The notion of Africa as a new land, the wave of the future, the start of a post-colonial order, is thus treated with scepticism and irony. Little is found to be new. Whereas slavery has come to be the symbol of European injustice to Africa, an injustice so great as to explain all the subsequent problems of Africa and of the descendants of the Africans in the Americas, *A Bend in the River* recalls the long history of slavery within Africa, the history of Arabs using African slaves (thus of the third world's own guilt), the privileged position of house slaves, the way slaves might feel more secure with a foreign master than freed among Africans of other tribes, the way as people interbred with their slaves they became indistinguishable from the slaves, until the former masters now indigenized became prey for the next strong conqueror who entered the scene. This vision, an essentially amoral concept of life as achievement and of the strong and weak, runs throughout Naipaul's work where it is often in contrast to the classical Indian – Hindu and Buddhist – notion of life as illusion, a place of suffering and experience. After his disillusionment with Yvette, Salim has an epiphany which seems the reverse of Camus' notion of life as

intensity of experience. It, significantly, occurs 'with the coming of
the light' at dawn, when 'the night had become part of the past':

> It seemed to me that men were born only to grow old, to live out
> their span, to acquire experience. Men lived to acquire experi-
> ence; the quality of the experience was immaterial; pleasure and
> pain – and above all, pain – had no meaning; to possess pain was
> as meaningless as to chase pleasure. And even when the illumi-
> nation vanished, became as thin and half nonsensical as a dream,
> I remembered that I had had it, that knowledge about the
> illusion of pain. (p. 229)

Before leaving London, Salim recalls this vision which now becomes an 'illumination' of 'men lost in space and time, but dread-
fully, pointlessly busy' (p. 248). Later, however, he compares 'That
illumination I held on to, about the unity of experience and the
illusion of pain' to Indar's sudden nostalgia for a 'home' that no
longer exists and calls it an Indian or Asiatic way of feeling, the
basis of an older way of life which they supposedly rejected, to
which there was no way of going back. Instead he vows to trample
on the past: 'We had become what the world outside had made us;
we had to live in the world as it existed' (p. 252).

If Indar and Salim learn to seize the day, and if, in the Hobbesian
world of social contracts, man makes himself through power, ruthlessness and achievement, there is always the possibility that this
too is an illusion and all activity is needless vanity. Life, as seen in
A Bend in the River, might be regarded as survival of the fittest; or it
might be a hell of recurring patterns of useless activity in which
nothing really changes and in which the history of Rome, the
British Empire and Africa are cycles of growth and decay. The
three rebellions in the novel may not be solely examples of an
African rage to return to an imagined former racial and tribal
purity, they may be part of an endless process of meaningless,
illusory history. In contrast to this there is also the human instinct
to achieve, to leave a mark in history, to be, in the vocabulary of
the novel, a man. Yet, as Indar learns by comparing himself to the
wealthy American, and as is shown by the contrast between London and the capital of the African state, or as is shown by the
limitations reality imposes on Mr Biswas' attempted rebellion, a
person's ability to accomplish and leave a mark on history is
limited by environment, by the past and achievements of the

culture. The existential is circumscribed by the material.

Besides the three rebellions and such recurring symbols as dark and light, houses and the water hyacinth, the contrasts between the two national capitals, there are numerous parallels, analogies, contrasts and structured ironies. In the parallels Naipaul's imagination can be seen as not only finding ironies but also attempting to examine the major themes and problems from different perspectives. Indar (like Naipaul himself) flees from a threatened Indian community to a famous university in England and attempts to become a self-made man, a cosmopolitan, international expert and advisor on third world problems, an intellectual independent of others. This is contrasted to Salim's quest for self-creation as a businessman, ironically the traditional role of Asiatics in the diaspora, in the heart of Africa. But Indar is found to be dependent on American foundations and wealth, and nostalgic for the now vanished home he fled. At the point Indar seems defeated by his awareness of his dependency, Salim's quest for independence and security takes him to London in another attempt to create a new life. There he finds many people like himself, aliens from former colonies, including Indians selling cigarettes on street corners (as the poor do in India and Africa). How are we to 'read' Salim's engagement in London to Kareisha, Nazruddin's daughter? While this fits into the Virgilian parallel, the fore-ordained marriage at the conclusion of the voyage upon which Rome will be built, it is, ironically, the kind of pre-arranged marriage within the East African Indian community from which Salim had originally fled.

A third quester is Nazruddin, a successful businessman, who knew when to flee Central Africa for Uganda and when to flee Uganda for Canada, but who finds himself in an equally ruthless world where he is cheated by other immigrants. His London apartments are filled with Arabs, East Europeans and small town English girls who do not pay him rent. London seems to consist of Arabs and other aliens on the streets seeking the jobs, opportunities, goods and safety not found in the places from which they come. Every place seems the same place. A similar orchestration of themes can be found in the parallel between Salim's affair with Yvette (which distracts him from the dangers of the political situation and results in his failing to sell his business and send money abroad before his business is nationalized) and the tight enclosed love marriage of Mahesh and Shoba (yet Mahesh, for all his obses-

sion with his relation to his wife, foresees the nationalization and
has sold his Bigburger – sign of the new American liberal imperialism – to an African employee).

Mahesh and Shoba represent the dangers of romantic love and,
as they are from different Indian castes, represent another version
of the forbidden mingling of races. The suggestion that the Arabs
of East Africa lost their idea of themselves and became weak, no
longer conquerors, by interbreeding with the Africans is in keeping with Indian notions of race and caste. It is the kind of idea
Salim might be expected to hold. It can also be seen as reflecting
the situation of the Indians and Arabs in East Africa, where after
independence African leaders said that such foreigners could stay
on only if they assimilated to the African community. In Zanzibar
Arab women were forced into marriage with Africans. Indian feelings of exclusiveness and racial fears are connected to Naipaul's
own fear of extinction, a fear which was expressed in terms of the
Indian being made extinct by creolization in the West Indies.

Naipaul has always been conscious of the difficulty of writing
about societies he does not know from the inside. *A Bend in the
River* is a book about Africa in which the lives, hopes and fears of
foreigners are central. It is as much about expatriates and diasporas
after decolonization as about national independence. That Naipaul
is of Indian descent and from the West Indies gives the novel a
different perspective from a book by Conrad or Greene, but it is
not a novel by a black African and its perspective must be different.
Bend, like *Guerrillas*, is partly an attempt to understand the problems that have followed from decolonization and partly a response
to unthinking slogans of the counterculture, New Left and other
fashions of the 1960s and early 1970s. That leaflet distributed by
the Liberation Army is a jumble of Marxist clichés, Fanonite calls
to violence, black nationalism and black consciousness – the representative confusion of several decades of anti-colonial and post-
colonial rhetoric of half-digested ideas often from outside Africa:

> . . . and since war is an extension of politics we have decided to
> face the ENEMY with armed confrontation. Otherwise we all die
> forever. The ancestors are shrieking. If we are not deaf we can
> hear them. By ENEMY we mean the powers of imperialism, the
> multinationals and the puppet powers that be, the false gods,
> the capitalists, the priests and teachers who give false interpreta-
> tions. The law encourages crime. The schools teach ignorance

and people practise ignorance in preference to their true culture. (p. 219)

That could have been written in London, San Francisco or Paris at
the time.

In fact a source was Argentina where Naipaul spent considerable
time between 1972 and 1977 examining how a formerly rich nation had degenerated into the destructive populist national-social-
ism of Perónism, political instability and the military government's
'dirty war' against the guerrillas. He interviewed guerrilla sympathizers and one of the movement's founders. Mimicry of the then
fashionable foreign notions of revolution had been grafted on to
the problems left by European colonialism, the mysticism of Perónist
nationalist cultural assertion and an attempted radical
decolonization. In an isolated area of northern Argentina, after
having seen police with machine guns in unmarked cars searching
for supposed guerrillas, he was a few days later taken from a bus,
detained, accused of being a guerrilla and threatened. He was told
that he had escaped torture and death only because the senior
police officer, fascinated by an African pipe Naipaul smoked, decided that he was a foreigner. His experience of the violent, irrational, guerrilla movement and the equally violent, irrational law-
lessness of the government's war against the guerrillas found its
way into A Bend in the River. 'I transferred . . . the emotion of
Argentina, and even the isolated police building in the bush of
Jujuy, to my Central African setting.'[48]

As often in Naipaul's writing there is an Indian subtext. The
title, A Bend in the River, suggests an analogy to the Indian classical
epic, the Ramayana. Manohar Malgonkar's novel A Bend in the
Ganges (1964), a love story set in the context of the Indian independence movement, independence and the horror of partition,
probably gave Naipaul the idea of applying the Rama story to the
problems resulting from decolonization. Malgonkar's novel begins with an epigraph from the Ramayana: 'At a bend in the
Ganges, they paused to look at the land they were leaving.'[49] Long
before the epics of Europe the Ramayana offers a story of voyage,
quest, exile, testing and return which is also a history of a people.
It might also be considered an early example of the literature of
imperialism as, according to some interpretations, it tells figura-
tively the Aryan expansion through the subcontinent, especially
through southern India and the fusion of the Aryans with the

Dravidians. Thus it would recall that imperialism has a much longer history there than in the West, that life repeats cycles of similar events, that long ago a light-skinned people conquered a dark-skinned people and from it formed India (with its continuing wheat-black colour distinctions). Naipaul could also have in mind the grandeur of the Aryan conquest with its supposedly ideal rule or the argument that the Aryans were seduced by India and then degenerated. Both visions – a view of imperial order and that the conquering people degenerates through interbreeding – are at times suggested by *Bend.*

Naipaul's novels have shown an evolving complexity as his vision has deepened and his imagination has become more powerful. Allusions and parallels are increasingly used to bring together associations he has in mind and as he has come to see his own experience as universal and not solely the result of colonial Trinidad. Such deepening and universalizing is common to writers as they mature and is especially characteristic of writers in self-exile. But Naipaul also belongs to a generation of writers who received their university education during a time when the use of myth and literary allusions by Joyce, Eliot and Yeats was in fashion. The *Ramayana* allows him to make use of his Indian heritage by rewriting the Rama story to fit an existential world without purpose. Yet this existential world is also an expression of the three aspects of Shiva as creation, continuity and destruction, the cyclical Indian view of history and reality. In *The Enigma of Arrival* (*EA*) Naipaul says that because he dreaded change he 'cultivated old, possibly ancestral ways of feeling . . . and held on to the idea of a world in flux: the drum of creation in the god's right hand, the flame of destruction in his left' (*EA*, p. 53).

Central to the *Ramayana* are Rama's fourteen years in exile from home. Along with his wife Sita and his half-brother Lakshmana (who acts as his servant), Rama crosses the Ganges and lives in a forest, symbolic of the world, populated by monkeys (usually understood to be a less advanced people who were allies of the Aryans). After Sita is kidnapped by demons and taken to Sri Lanka where she is imprisoned, Hanuman, the monkey god, discovers her for Rama, who must go to Lanka and fight and kill Ravana, leader of the demons. Fearing his wife has been dishonoured, Rama rejects Sita until she can prove her purity by a trial of fire; then Rama returns home from his exile to claim his throne and institutes a perfect reign.

Naipaul uses various motifs from and alludes to the structure of the epic. The relevant allusions or ironies are the meetings of peoples (Aryans, monkeys, Lankans – Europe, Asians, Africa), Rama's exile in the forest (Salim and Indar in Central Africa and London), a servant (Lakshmana, Metty), wife and purity (Kareisha and, ironically, Yvette), Rama's years in the forest (Salim's ten in central Africa), the monkeys (which in this novel are smoked and eaten by the Africans), Lanka (the Big Man's capital), Hanuman's voyage to Lanka to find Sita (Salim goes to London to become engaged), the battle between good and evil as represented by Rama and Ravana (ironically the apocalyptical battle breaking out at the end of the novel between the Big Man and the 'Fanonites', itself analogous to the Book of Revelation), the trial of Sita's purity (Salim would have formerly been concerned that Kareisha may no longer be virgin). But whereas Rama goes home again and insti-tutes a perfect reign, Salim knows, unlike Indar, that in the mod-ern world there is no going back, there is no home. There is also no battle between Good and Evil, only between the Big Man's mimicry of European order and those wanting to return to the purity of the African past. There is no seat of imperial order, only the disorder of contemporary London. This is the only world we have, a world in which to create, experience and leave our mark. 'The world is what it is; men who are nothing, who allow them-selves to become nothing, have no place in it.'

A Bend in the River was one of the major works of fiction concern-ing the problems of freedom written while Naipaul was living in a rented cottage in Wiltshire after his return to England following his disillusioning experience with *The Loss of El Dorado*. The auto-biographical dimension, including the ways in which he incorpo-rated into the novel his English surroundings and his awareness of the way life changes and people need to create their identity, can be found in *The Enigma of Arrival*.

9

Finding the Centre, The Enigma of Arrival, A Turn in the South and India: A Million Mutinies

He had never before, I think, made a connected narrative out of those little stories. (*India: A Million Mutinies*, p. 202)

Naipaul's writing began to change again in the early 1980s. This new mood first appeared in the 'two narratives' of *Finding the Centre* (1984). The title is significant of the way the relation of the writer's self to his work is now accepted as the answer to the problems of marginality, exile and insecurity that characterized his earlier books. The centre is now the creation and discovery of the self rather than external in an ideal society. Recognition that the problems of Trinidad, India and England are similar and that all life is subject to change was followed by a new mellowness. There are still moments of irritability, but such eruptions are brief and followed by what may seem a too tolerant interest. Women also begin to appear in the books as enjoyable friends rather than as dangers who mislead men from their work.

The 'Author's Foreword' to *Finding the Centre* is reminiscent of a preface by Henry James in his late period. Naipaul tells us that both narratives are 'about the process of writing', discusses how the idea of the pieces came about and what constitutes 'the centre of the narrative' (p. 10). The long complex train of thought and movement of the prose, especially in the fourth paragraph of the 'Foreword', feels Jamesian. The centre of the narrative (the core idea rather than the story) is intertwined with the author in middle

136

age coming to understand his beginnings and, with others he meets, and to whom he is attracted, 'trying to find order in their world, looking for the centre' (p. 10). Many of Naipaul's previous books, such as *Among the Believers: An Islamic Journey* (1981), were concerned with people seeking or claiming to have found centres, but the results were disappointing, disillusioning, a new disorder. Usually the centre was an idealized past, a rejection of the Enlightenment, tolerance and rationality. From now on Naipaul's books will be more populated with sympathetic characters, and the disillusionments of the past will be recognized as at least in part a projection of his own inner world, a using of previous experience as a guide to other minds and lands:

> A writer after a time carries his world with him, his own burden of experience, human experience and literary experience (one deepening the other); and I do believe – especially after writing 'Prologue to an Autobiography' – that I would have found equivalent connections with my past and myself wherever I had gone. (p. 10)

The writer carries his world (including in Naipaul's case a sense of disorder and a need for order) within himself, but only finds the truth about himself in the process of writing. There has always been such an autobiographical, confessional layer in Naipaul's work, along with the need to build upon, order and analyse facts and experience. There has always been the temptation to merge literary genres, to mix autobiography, self-analysis, fiction, facts, reportage, social and cultural analysis, to create a meta-narrative which would explain the various influences on how it came into being. *A House for Mr Biswas* and *The Mimic Men* are as much steps in this direction as the diary entries in *In a Free State*. Jimmy's diary-fiction in *Guerrillas* is another exploration of the true and inauthentic dynamics of writing as are the various books supposedly written by Pundit Ganesh in *The Mystic Masseur*.

Naipaul has moved into a new phase when the pains and insecurities of the past, such as the need to travel to find subject matter to write about, are admitted to be a source of discovery and pleasure, an opening of a world of experience and insight, a process that he now celebrates, a history which in itself is to be ordered into narrative and through which he discovers and creates a new self. 'However creatively one travels, however deep an experience in childhood or middle age, it takes thought (a shifting of impulses, ideas and references that become more multifarious as one grows older) to understand what one has lived through or where one has been' (p. 12).

While 'Prologue to an Autobiography' offers more information about Naipaul's early life than was previously available, the narrative has a complicated structure, moving back and forth in time, its chronological tale being revealed through circles of memories. As the narrative moves forward it often moves back into time before rejoining the present at the conclusion. Naipaul has previously used such unusual, seemingly free, but highly organized narratives – in *The Mimic Men* for example – and the influences can equally be Proust or the complex organization of Indian story-telling as contemporary literary fashion. This, as well as realism, seems Naipaul's natural mode.

The Enigma of Arrival (1987) is another of Naipaul's controversial novels. A theme of the novel is that each person has a different perspective, a unique vision, as a result of individual experience. Each person has his or her own story. (This is rather different from contemporary literary theorists who believe that all writing is a history of domination and resistance by groups.) The narrator arrives on a rainy day in a village in Wiltshire and meticulously describes what he sees and discovers as he eventually begins to feel at ease in his rented cottage and its surroundings. From the start we are aware that the narrator, originally from Trinidad, has been unrooted, wandering, for many years, without feeling at home and is disillusioned and depressed. As he begins to understand where he is, he also realizes that his notions of and associations with his new home have been wrongly influenced by his colonial education and readings in English literature. He must learn to see anew, to understand what he is actually seeing rather than what he expects to see. Again and again his perceptions are found to be wrong. No sooner has he corrected one mistake than the correction needs to be corrected by further information or someone else's point of view. People and places need to be seen in context and studied to get at the truth; but the people, places and contexts keep changing. Understanding is a continual process of correction; narrative is made from giving order to the attempt to understand. There is a double focus throughout the novel – what is being described and the self-conscious awareness of the act of trying to see correctly.

Very early on the narrator speaks of his tropic island and of

Trinidad, thus making us aware that he is both a fictional character and autobiographical. Increasingly we become aware that the
narrator is Naipaul and that the life in Trinidad and London, the
books and trips abroad, arc his own. This is not clear at first
because the narrator refers to the personal in a distancing manner
as if his past were fiction, something imagined by an author as
background. By the last section of the book the distance between
narrator and author collapses as we are told how the book came to
be written. Still the question remains, are all the people and events
described real, are some derived from real people, or imagined?
What is the relationship of the people Naipaul describes to actual
people? As the characters have figurative significances, they are at
least partly imagined.

In *The Enigma of Arrival* Naipaul has revised a well known form of
early modernist fiction, the autobiographical novel. The relationship of the autobiographical to the fictional is given aesthetic
distance and the origins of the novel are explained by the autobiographical. Characteristics shared by *Enigma* with modernist autobiographical novels by Proust, Mann and Joyce include the developing sensitivity and awareness of the artist, the alienation of the
artist, the circularity of the form (so that the conclusion leads back
to the beginning), the role of memory in recovering the past, the
multiple time scheme that memory imposes on the narrative, the
continual revealing of realities to be illusions, the unusual position
of the narrator in relationship to the story, the privileging of art as
a means of arresting the flux of the world and giving life significance, and the originality of the novel in comparison to its models.

Naipaul is writing during an era when the artist and art are no
longer considered sacred and when the continuing relevance of
the novel form itself has been questioned by Naipaul among others. Moreover Naipaul's writing has always had an unusual relationship to the traditions of the European novel, both building
upon its models and critically revising them in terms of his own
experience of the colonial and post-colonial world. Like *A House
for Mr Biswas* or *A Bend in the River*, *The Enigma of Arrival* uses,
parodies and replies to earlier European literary forms. While
retaining some of the ambiguity of the relationship of the story to
the autobiographical, it makes the relationship much clearer than
in most novels of this kind and could be said to be demonstration
of how such a novel comes into existence, while at the same time
occupying an ambiguous space between autobiography and fic-

tion. The early fiction of Jean Rhys has a similar blurring of diary
and fiction. The closeness of personal experience to what the
writer writes about is a central theme of *Enigma* and of Naipaul's
later poetics. The novel is, even more than the two narratives of
Finding the Centre, a self-conscious demonstration of the various
sources of his writings. Naipaul draws attention to how his books
came to be written. There is the psychological need to be a writer,
a desire given him by his father's ambitions and strengthened by
his British West Indian colonial education and by a preference for
solitude in reaction to the disorderly extended family of Naipaul's
youth. There was the basic fracture, uprooting from the family and
the Indian Trinidadian community and the life of expatriation,
necessary to pursue a career as a writer. This includes the impoverished struggle of his early days in London, subsequent financial
disillusionments and insecurities as well as the basic insecurity of
being an alien in England – a foreigner of different skin colour,
from a different cultural background, someone who could not
easily blend into society. For the expatriate there is always a feeling
of disillusionment, of not being at home, of no longer having a
home. For the third world colonial there is always awareness of
difference, of being seen and treated differently. Such feelings
remained with Naipaul until the time of *The Enigma of Arrival*.
Besides feeling a foreigner in Wiltshire, there is his feeling that he
is an accident of imperial history – an Indian earning a living as a
writer in English in England – and his view that his own life is part
of a larger historical process which began with the sending of
indentured Indian labourers to Trinidad.

This novel then is more than autobiographical; its themes of
decay, change, flux, exile, solitude, individual will and ways of
seeing are parts of a larger concern with how humanity makes
itself, with how individuals adapt and create, with ambition, exploration, self-assertion, achievement and death. The interweaving of
such themes, like the interweaving of the autobiographical and
the novelistic, is musical, like the musical-spatial organization of
the great modernist literary works of the first half of the century.

Enigma differs from earlier models in that the world the narrator
describes in the fictional sections is a society he enters in middle
age. From internal evidence he is forty years old when he first
comes to the cottage. He is about fifty when he leaves for the house
he has built by reconditioning two other cottages. In such novels
or sequences of novels the illusions of youth and young adulthood

are deflated or seen in a new perspective as the narrator matures and can look back on the past. But, as Naipaul has said, he has no mature social experience he can write about; his first four novels were based on his early life in Trinidad; his later novels were the result of bringing his Trinidadian experience to observations of the third world. He could not write about English society without inventing a world of which he was not part. *Enigma* uses the conventions of the novel of social discriminations, with its disillusionments with former appearances, to learn to understand an alien society which is figurative of learning how to see life correctly instead of with the distorted perspectives of a colonial youth or a disillusioned writer in mid-career. Throughout the novel there is emphasis on seeing and understanding. On the first page: 'I could hardly see', 'I saw', 'all that I saw', 'This idea of winter', 'as I had imagined', 'was a blur to me', 'hard for me to distinguish', 'I didn't associate', 'I liked to look', 'I noticed', 'I remembered'.

Naipaul explains how he brought emotions he felt in Wiltshire to books he was writing at the time, such as *In a Free State* and *A Bend in the River*. *In a Free State*, for example, can now be seen as not only based on Naipaul's earlier experiences in East and Central Africa; it also reflects the disillusionment and insecurity which followed the writing of *The Loss of El Dorado*. Naipaul, homeless, feeling trapped by the need to earn his living as a writer in alien England, projected the ironies of freedom and expatriation on to his Europeans in Africa. Their disillusioning exile and frightened journey was influenced by his own since leaving Trinidad.

Enigma is not only about its own creation but, along with 'Prologue to an Autobiography', concerns the origins of Naipaul's other works. The general movement of his writing can be seen to have progressed from memories of Trinidad, an unsettling period of discontent and attempts to flee England (*An Area of Darkness* to *The Loss of El Dorado*), a decade of taking root in Wiltshire while writing about the third world, followed by his recent books concerned with the sources and act of writing. Naipaul early felt he had been born into a period of decay when the world had passed its peak; Trinidad, England and India lacked the grandeur he had idealized and had come to expect of the world from his reading and education. Then to avoid disappointment and further mental hurt he trained himself to see the world as a place of change and flux with decay being part of recurring cycles. His model was

Indian philosophy in which creation and destruction are different aspects of the same god. The vision of history consisting of conquests and the rise and fall of empires in *A Bend in the River* is infused as much by Indian thought as by the existential assertion of man making himself. Although Naipaul does not say so, it is this existential theme which recurs in still other guises in the later writing. *Enigma* is both about Naipaul making himself as a writer and a celebration of the Indian diaspora. 'Every generation now was to take us further away from those sanctities. But we remade the world for ourselves.' He sees 'life and man as the mystery, the true religion of men, the grief and the glory' (p. 318).

The Enigma of Arrival can be seen as a rewriting and fulfilment of *A House for Mr Biswas*. Like the earlier novel it is a record of the Indian diaspora as exemplified by the life of the Naipauls and their family relations. Again we return to the father–son, Biswas–Anand, relationship and allusions are made to Naipaul's own past in Trinidad and to such events mentioned in the 'epilogue' to *Biswas* as his father's debts and Naipaul's failure to return home from England for his father's illness and death. *Enigma* is structurally similar to *Biswas*. The first half of the book is similarly a record of seeming failure. Naipaul, like Biswas, has moved from house to house without taking root, has failed to gain the independence and security he wants, has invested his hopes in a major project which ends in disaster and mental distress. He unwillingly returns to England beaten by life, just as Biswas, suffering from a mental breakdown, returned to the Tulsi house he had tried to escape. He, like Biswas, must start again; and like Biswas in Port of Spain the narrator's life in Wiltshire is a healing process leading to success. Biswas' story concludes with the obtaining of a house of his own; the narrator's story also leads to the building of his own house. Both novels end with family deaths and in *Biswas* with a celebration of the father's painful achievement, in *Enigma* with a celebration of the son's achievement. Both novels have circular structures with the conclusion explaining how each book was written by the narrator from personal or family events. Both novels can be seen as structured in two equal halves with an epilogue.

Enigma concludes the story of *Biswas*. The son acts out a similar drama of attempting to make a mark on history, is for a time bewildered and defeated by the challenges of freedom, is mentally hurt, but eventually finds a suitable place where he experiences renewal, a second life, flourishes and after a time purchases his own house. While the first novel is primarily of pain and small victories, the later novel is more fully a celebration of how: 'We had made made ourselves anew. The world we had found ourselves in . . . was one we had partly made ourselves, and had longed for' (p. 317). Both novels are about the will to survive, achieve, rise in the world; both are about the struggle for dignity, the right to individuality, the painful making of oneself and with it the celebration of family and community, the assertion and creation of a place in history, the defeat of extinction, the defeat of the void.

The Enigma of Arrival is described on the title page as 'A novel in five sections'. The formal structure consists of 41 subsections or chapters divided almost equally between the book's two halves with the fifth section as an epilogue. The organization of sections and chapters is I.12, II.7; III.12, IV.9; V.1. The two halves of the novel are almost equal in length, sections I and II consisting of 152 pages while sections III, IV and V take 151 pages. The centre of the novel in terms of length is: 'With me, everything started from writing. Writing had brought me to England, had sent me away from England; had given me a vision of romance; had nearly broken me with disappointment. Now it was writing, the book, that gave savour, possibility to each day . . .' (p. 154). At the centre of *Enigma* the narrator recounts leaving Gloucester for Wiltshire and alludes to the opening of the novel 'For the first four days it rained and was misty; I could hardly see where I was' (p. 154). The novel starts over again with many of the original scenes recalled in what might be described as a musical recapitulation.

While *Enigma* has several intertwined formal structures, including the gradual pulling together of selective fragmentary allusions into an autobiographical chronology and a discussion of the author's previous writings, its basic structural principles are musical – the development and echoing of various recurring motifs and themes within and across formal structures – and perspectivism, the retelling or revisioning in new ways and contexts of what was earlier described. The landscape, weather, characters, gardens, houses and the narrator keep being redescribed as they change or are seen in a new light. Such themes as death, time, change, freedom, dependency, seeing, knowing, illness, age, continuity, building, order, chaos and migration keep recurring.

Each of the five sections has its own musical key, a symbol such as the ambiguous nature of Jack's garden or the destructive effect of the attractive ivy, around which the themes, descriptions and events circle, depart and return. Memory and association allow transformations of motifs and modulations of key. Brief allusions allow motifs to be gradually introduced or to recur. There is counterpoint or fugal development when different stories, characters and themes are taken up, dropped, recur or are juxtaposed with other stories, characters and themes.

Section I concludes with a celebration of Jack:

> He was not exactly a remnant; he had created his own life, his own world, almost his own continent. . . . he had created a garden on the edge of a swamp and a ruined farmyard: had responded to and found glory in the seasons. All around him was ruin; and all around, in a deeper way, was change, and a reminder of the brevity of the cycles of growth and creation. But he had sensed that life and man were the true mysteries; and he had asserted the primacy of these with something like religion. The bravest and most religious thing about his life was his way of dying. (p. 87)

This is the vision with which Naipaul concludes the novel; it also anticipates the very words and themes of Section V ('we remade the world for ourselves . . . death . . . showed me life and man as the mystery and true religion of men' [p. 318]).

The recurrence of themes and symbols is usually musical – in the return of words, phrases, symbols – and felt to be part of a rich patterning of sounds, images, allusions and associations: it is also seen in the way the novel keeps returning to the rainy days of Naipaul's first arrival in Wiltshire and the foregrounded symbolism of its title, 'The Enigma of Arrival'. At first we are told that the title refers to a painting by Chirico about which Naipaul had thought to write a short story (pp. 91–2). Naipaul's original dismissive description of Chirico's other paintings might indeed be the casual reader's first hasty impression of *Enigma* as a novel: 'arbitrary assemblages, in semi-classical, semi-modern settings, of unrelated motifs – aqueducts, trains, arcades, gloves, fruit, statues – with an occasional touch of easy mystery' (p. 91). We are told that this one painting, 'The Enigma of Arrival', kept changing in Naipaul's memory. But even before Naipaul begins to offer his first version of the story it is associated with the opening of his novel and his arrival in Wiltshire: 'And in the winter grey of the manor grounds in Wiltshire, in those first four days of mist and rain, when so little was clear to me an idea – floating lightly above the book I was working on – came to me of a story I might one day write about that scene in the Chirico picture' (p. 92). While the first version of the story might be interpreted as based on Naipaul's trip to and flight from India in *An Area of Darkness* ('something like an Indian bazaar scene') it is also obviously applicable to 'In a Free State'. ('. . . that Mediterranean story was really no more than a version of the story I was already writing' [p. 93].)

Soon, however, the journey motif gathers to itself a wide body of associations such as the description of the basic themes of *The Loss of El Dorado* ('discovery, the New World . . .' [p. 94]) and of Naipaul's life since leaving Trinidad (pp. 95–7). Within a few pages the theme of a journey to a foreign land from which one cannot return becomes symbolic of Naipaul's life and life itself, both for the migrant (Naipaul's return to Trinidad in 1970, after writing the 'romance' of *The Loss of El Dorado* coincides with the Black Power demonstrations) and for anyone faced by change, the passing of time and death: 'his life's journey – had been made' (p. 157). Still later, at the novel's conclusion, the journey motif is applied to the Indian diaspora and his family: 'There was no ship of antique shape now to take us back. We had come out of the nightmare; and there was nowhere else to go' (p. 317). The ship-wrecked image of *The Mimic Men* has been revised with a happier ending. In its rich musicality and formal complexity *The Enigma of Arrival* continues the modernist tradition of T. S. Eliot's *Four Quartets* and James Joyce's *Finnegans Wake*, but it revises such forms for the concerns of the post-colonial world and for the more open, autobiographical manner of post-modernism.

There are two interwoven themes in *Enigma* suggesting that Naipaul's time in Wiltshire on the estate has an allegorical dimension. The landlord and his estate are associated with imperial England. Their history is the history of modern England. The landlord's sloth and preoccupation with his past have led to decay, the loss of order in his estate and the emergence of new people, including Naipaul, as important. Naipaul's presence on the estate and reconversion of a property into his own house reverses the imperial story of the indentured Indian labourer on the Trinidadian sugar plantation, yet ironically the situation of Naipaul working at his writing on an English estate has its parallels to the past. Like the sugar plantation owner who was absent from Trinidad, living in England, and like the imperial government which has withdrawn to its own local problems, the local estate owner has withdrawn into his memories. He has let the estate (state – Trinidad, Empire, England's historical culture) become an economic burden and is eventually displaced by an energetic, new post-war lower and middle-class order that includes foreigners and former colonials. Jack is part of a new order, a new England which pretends to carry on older traditions.

The estate and the lands near it are also symbolic of English literature, bringing to the narrator's mind a range of English writing from medieval English literature to the present. It seems from the landlord and Alan that English literature has also decayed – only a novelist friend of the narrator who scrupulously observes society is to be trusted – and the implications are that Naipaul is now, ironically, the heir of the imperial language and literature. Like the Rooks (an old-fashioned image of blacks) Naipaul and other former colonials have taken over part of England and English literature. It is the figurative representation of the decay of the imperial order and the rise of the post-colonial that makes it unlikely that the people and world observed by the narrator are always factually real. The disruption of the fictional and distanced with the factual and undisguised personal is what makes *Enigma* post-modern, post-colonial.

Throughout *Enigma* Naipaul touches upon his relationship to European cultural traditions, especially in the arts. They, as well as Indian culture, made him, but such an education was mimicry, learning without understanding or, because alien to his experience, distorting and the source of fantasies. The narrator sees the shearing of sheep and it is 'like something out of an old novel, perhaps by Hardy, or out of a Victorian country diary' (p. 18). Jack at first appears 'as in a version of a Book of Hours' (p. 20). 'Jack's father-in-law . . . seemed a Wordsworthian figure . . . going gravely about his peasant tasks, as if in an immense Lake District solitude' (p. 20). In Trinidad Naipaul had imagined Dickens' novels to be populated with a cast of multiracial characters similar to the society he knew. Often the world he read about in English literature was baffling, words did not correspond to their use in Trinidad. The English countryside became the pastoral scenes of cows on a tin of milk or some idealized landscape reproduced on a painting. When he first went to England as a student and aspiring writer he was baffled and depressed by the actuality; there was no grand

imperial land of continuous traditions awaiting him with open
arms, his life was pinched, among other immigrants, and he was
surrounded by what appeared to be decay and ruin. Like other
colonial students from the third world he felt humiliated, a per-
petual outsider, but unlike most others he had cut his ties with the
past and felt he had a vocation to be a writer, a career he could
undertake only in England. He could not write the smart sophisticated novel of an experienced man of the world or the novel of
refined inner sensibility which he admired and which was a product of the security and wealth of imperial England. He had to
discover that only his own life and experience could be the basis of
his subject matter and themes. Which *Enigma* is.

Towards the conclusion of Section II, 'The Journey', Naipaul
returns to a subject he has treated in previous books, especially in
The Mimic Men, the months he spent in an Earls Court boarding
house when he first arrived in England, before going to Oxford.
Naipaul's sexual and social innocence do not appear abnormal for
someone of his age at that time. Nor does his inability to have
appreciated, when he was eighteen years old, that the 'true material of the boarding house' was the 'flotsam of Europe not long
after the end of the terrible war' or that he himself 'was at the
beginning of that great movement of peoples that was to take
place in the second half of the twentieth century – a movement
and cultural mixing greater than the peopling of the United States'
(p. 130). What is, however, striking about his discussion of the past
is the clarity, economy and precision with which he turns this
particular enigma of arrival into a statement about his methods as
an artist. 'Unwilling as a writer ever to fabricate, to invent where I
had no starting-point of knowledge' (p. 129). '[I]f I had noted
down simply what I had seen' (p. 131), if he had the 'security' to
take an interest in people, talk to them and ask questions (p. 131).
Writing requires material, an idea, a story, a setting, dialogue,
themes, a model, interest in others, a sense of inquiry, an ability to
see, practice.

Enigma has its share of false writers. There is Alan, who does
some newspaper reviews and talks on cultural topics on the radio
and whose very brightness and trendiness confuses received ideas
of cultural stylishness with being an artist. He dies without writing
a book. More interesting is the landlord of the manor, who is a
minor artist and poet in an older style deriving from late nineteenth-century aestheticism. He might be regarded as an embodi-

ment of England's Edwardian imperial power and security which allowed its artists to turn inward from external realities to refinements of feeling, eroticism and playfulness. The wealth that built the manor allows him to withdraw into himself as the estate decays. The ivy that he loves eventually overruns and destroys the buildings. He has published a book at his own expense. He is the opposite of Naipaul and might be understood as figurative of the decay and eventual end of a formerly influential British literary tradition which Naipaul at first tried to imitate and found to be unsuitable for himself and his times. Naipaul living and writing on the estate represents the start of a new direction in English literature, the former colonial who will build his own house by radically redesigning and converting the buildings of the past to his own uses.

The Enigma of Arrival is less a story of Naipaul's becoming English and assimilating to English literary traditions than a claim to have come, eventually taken root, and in his own way, conquered. It is not really a story of acculturation and assimilation; rather it implies that Naipaul and other former colonials are now part of, and inheritors of, the English literary tradition. It continues a history that started with the English conquest of India. It is a daring claim. To have set his story in London would have been less daring.

Cities like London were to change. They were to cease being more or less national cities; they were to become cities of the world, modern-day Romes . . . They were to be cities visited for learning and elegant goods and manners and freedom by all the barbarian peoples of the globe, people of forest and desert, Arabs, Africans, Malays. (p. 130)

But to have set his story in rural England, the England of Hardy's novels, of Constable's paintings, of Cowper's verses and Victorian diaries, of Stonehenge, and to have contrasted his successful career as a writer and his conversion of local houses to his own design with the decay and disorder of the manor and the failure of Alan and his landlord as writers, with their notions of a literature of sensibility, is in a way to declare oneself the inheritor, someone who has not only earned his place but who is part of the new order, the new literary tradition of the migration of the world's people. From a British or American perspective that much overused word post-colonial means the collapse of a tradition and cultural fragmentation as a result of internationalism, cultural relativism and cultural pluralism. For critics who take that view there are no more novels, only voices, voices from the margin demanding to be heard. But if I understand *The Enigma of Arrival,* Biswas' children, after much hard work and learning to adapt what they have found on their journeys, do have a house, and it is in the very heart of the English literary tradition which has been reconverted and redesigned to tell and celebrate their story. This novel is about such changes and their causes.

Naipaul's struggle to create order, as a writer and for his own emotional needs, from historical change and the chaotic freedom of the present is continually in conflict with a longing for stability, rootedness and continuity. His love of landscape, noticeable especially in his recent books, is in part a desire for harmony with his surroundings, while his awareness of the seasons could be understood as a way of transforming the flux of the actual world into orderly, continuous cycles of change. *A Turn in the South* compassionately examines people with a similar desire for wholeness and harmony. Naipaul had previously shown a reserve towards the United States, which he associated with racial discrimination, cultural crudeness and imperialism. Americans replace the departing Europeans in *Guerrillas* and *A Bend in the River* as the new world order of junk food, big business and the world's police when local disorder threatens Western interests. As happens with many people from the Commonwealth, England is the country and culture towards which he has had ambivalent feelings while the United States, especially the South, was the land of racial discrimination (of a radical kind not found in England), of lynching and of the Ku Klux Klan. Naipaul has always made a clear distinction between the condition of black Americans, a powerless, victimized minority, and the self-governing black African or West Indian. This is especially true of Trinidad where slavery lasted less than fifty years and where the Indians were brought in to work the sugar plantations. Yet, curiously, the American South was in the past linked to the West Indies. Such islands as Barbados and Antigua had rich sugar plantation economies, and were places of opportunities, at a time when much of the South was still frontier.

In *A Turn in the South* (1989) Naipaul re-examines his former prejudice towards the southern United States. As in *The Enigma of Arrival* he tries to see and understand a place that he had previously understood through received ideas. He wants to understand the South's resistance to modernization and its pride in its culture when the culture was built upon the horror of slavery. How had the black southerner learned to survive and adapt? Naipaul is impressed by the role of religion in helping people make sense of their lives and in providing a feeling of community and service. People are allowed to speak for themselves and there are conflicting voices usually presented without judgement. At times Naipaul appears starry-eyed, more concerned with finding links between his own past in Trinidad and the ways of the South than with analysis. But that is part of trying to see reality freshly – as when he attempts to see Mississippian history through the eyes of the whites, or when he uncritically accepts someone's mythology of the redneck – and his recent delight with the world around him. Naipaul, now conscious of death, enjoys other ways of seeing and being than those that had governed his feelings in the past. Increasingly these later books are concerned with other people and what their situation has in common with his own. How have they learned to adapt? Just as he uncritically accepts an idealization of the redneck as trying to live the free life of a frontiersman, so almost every black character in the book is admirable except for the few who are obviously emotionally disturbed and unreliable. But then the theme of *A Turn in the South* is 'home'. What does it feel like to live in a part of the modern world where people can speak of 'home' and what enables the Southerners, white and black, to have such feelings?

Naipaul's third book of Indian travels, *India: A Million Mutinies* (*MM*) (1991), is written with his earlier Indian books in mind and is another revision, another re-seeing of what had been wrongly judged in the past. Even the structure, the crowds of Bombay at the start of his Indian adventure and the Kashmiri hotel, recalls *An Area of Darkness*. It is, like his other recent books, well populated, filled with the voices of a wide variety of people who are allowed to speak for themselves without much authorial commentary. Opinions, views, possible solutions are allowed to clash. The interest is more in what has created such voices than in imposing an order. Where Naipaul formerly sought a tradition but found decay and chaos, now he has come to accept that life consists of change and to find interest in the ways that people strive to change their lives for the better. In the twenty-seven years between his first visit to India and his current one, Naipaul and the India he observes have changed in analogous ways. They have changed from the confusions that accompanied independence to the many voices and perspectives of the post-colonial.

In 1962 Naipaul was still humiliated by his colonial past in Trinidad, a humiliation that he blamed on India, where notions of greatness had been lost among pettiness. For centuries foreigners had conquered and ruled India because of its own internal weaknesses. What had been one of the world's greatest civilizations stopped developing, became backward, inward, fragmented, ready for conquest, its people superstitious, passive, impoverished, sent abroad as indentured labour. In 1962, seeking to find his cultural home in India, he discovered he was not part of the family he imagined, he did not belong to the local clans, he did not have the local vision. Instead of national independence bringing renewal he found poverty, feudal caste attitudes, fatalism, lack of rationality and a failure of vision.

Returning to India during a time when others fear the collapse of the Indian central state because of regional, caste and religious conflicts, Naipaul finds signs of vitality and renewal. There is now a new wealth, a new national economy controlled by Indians and not by foreigners. Many people are prosperous and others can hope to improve their conditions. Notions of freedom and self-assertion have moved from the elite to a broader range of society. A notion of India has been restored, after having been lost for centuries, and it is this sense of identity which is being challenged by further claims for recognition.

Naipaul sees such renewal as beginning with the peace the British had imposed on India after the mutiny of 1857. Until then the country was the victim of repeated Muslim invasions and was divided among various groups who, because of local politics, had taken sides with foreign invaders. British rule brought unity and began a period of scholarship which reconstructed a sense of national identity, led to the nationalist movement and independence. Notions of freedom continued to develop and, supported by recent economic changes, created the energy and demands for recognition that characterize the present: 'To awaken to history was to cease to live instinctively . . . it was to know a kind of rage . . . every group thought itself unique in its awakening; and every group sought to separate its rage from rage of other groups' (p. 420).

An older generation of nationalists needed to find a usable past and folk tradition which they asserted against the culture of their colonizers; but such traditionalism became reactionary, even an absurd humiliation, after independence. Naipaul's continuing exploration of the paradoxes of freedom is both more suitable for the post-colonial world and a further stage in the process of decolonization. In his recognition of how British imperialism made possible the creation of a modern India we might, in the West, find a clue how to see our own problems concerning the role of European imperial history, our canon of literature and our cultural ideas in contemporary multicultural societies.

Naipaul's writing has moved with our era from the confusions of decolonization, with its suspicions, humiliations, and continuing dependency, to what is often termed the post-colonial, a joyful acceptance of the energies, cultural achievements, conflicting claims and freedoms that have resulted from independence along with the increased wealth, transportation and communication of recent decades. Although Naipaul's writings are a record and analysis of such changes there is a subtext – the soil from which they have been nourished is himself:

> Cruelty, yes it was in the nature of Indian family life. The clan that gave protection and identity, and saved people from the void, was itself a little state, and it could be a hard place, full of politics, full of hatreds, and changing alliances and moral denunciations. It was the kind of family life I had known for much of my childhood: an early introduction to the ways of the world, and to the nature of cruelty. It had given me . . . a taste for the other kind of life, the solitary or less crowded life, where one had space around oneself. (I: *MM*, p. 178)

Appendix A

Naipaul's Family, *A House for Mr Biswas* and *The Mimic Men*

As Naipaul dislikes writing about the unfamiliar his fiction makes imaginative use of actual people and events. His sources are useful to understand the autobiographical implications of the novels. His father Seepersad (b. 1906) is the model for Mr Biswas. After Seepersad's father died when he was six years old, Seepersad and his impoverished mother became dependent on his mother's sister (the novel's Tara) and her wealthy husband (Ajodha) who owned rum shops, taxis and other businesses. After some schooling Seepersad became a sign-painter; he painted a sign for the general store connected to Lion House (Hanuman House) owned by the Capildeos (the Tulsis) of Chaguanas and married Bropatie Capildeo (Shama). Although his children were born in Lion House he usually resided elsewhere. After he had painted advertising signs for the *Trinidad Guardian* (the *Sentinel*), the editor allowed him to submit articles, then hired him as a reporter. As Seepersad had a highly developed sense of humour his reports and interviews made him well known. After several moves he became the newspaper's Chaguanas correspondent but lived by himself in a wooden house away from Lion House until he had a mental collapse – possibly influenced by his resignation from the paper after the editor had been fired and its policy changed, and possibly by a fierce quarrel with the very orthodox Hindu Capildeos about religious reform. After his nervous breakdown he became an overseer on a Capildeo estate (Green Vale) and then a shopkeeper (The Chase). He rejoined the *Guardian,* and moved to Port of Spain where for ten years he lived in various houses owned by the

Capildeos before acquiring his own house (the Sikkim Street house). He spent three years with a new Department of Social Welfare, after which the Department was abolished and he returned again to the *Guardian*, although he lost his pension rights. He died of a heart attack during 1953 when V. S. Naipaul was studying in England.

The Capildeos descended from a minor Indian aristocrat and pundit who was kidnapped in Calcutta and sent to Trinidad as an indentured labourer. There he married Rosalie Soogee Gobin (Mrs Tulsi) with whom he had nine daughters and two sons before he died (1925). Rudranath (Owad), the younger son, attended Queen's Royal College, where he was (like Ganesh in *The Mystic Masseur*) for a time, as a rural Indian, a misfit who studied hard but did not do well, and after graduation taught. He (Owad again) went to university in England where he was elected head of several student organizations, read the *Statesman* and became an avid supporter of Soviet Communism. He returned to Trinidad where he lived with his mother while he and his elder brother, Sambhoonath (Shekhar) became involved in one of the new political parties (various details are used in *The Mystic Masseur* where Rudranath is a source for Indrasingh). Rudranath returned to England, for post-graduate research, then became the leader of the Democratic Labour Party when the Trinidadian opposition needed a well known educated Indian to oppose Eric Williams' People's National Movement. Although predominantly Indian the DLP was multiracial and for a time included Uriah Butler and Albert Gomes among its leadership. Because of its mixed racial leadership, most of whom were the older, flamboyant, independent politicans, it was also unstable and when an Indian quit in 1957 Butler declared that all Indians were traitors. Rudranath (the Ralph Singh of *The Mimic Men*) was wealthy, politically ineffective, divided his time between England and Trinidad, wrote spiritualistic autobiographies (like *The Mystic Masseur* and Singh in *The Mimic Men*) but won a majority in the 1958 election. As Williams saw his PNM leading Trinidad to independence and hoped to head a Caribbean federation, both of which the Indians opposed as leading to black domination, he accused the Indians of treason, of being a 'hostile and recalcitrant minority', the 'greatest danger facing the country', and violence followed. The 1961 elections, which the PNM won, were particularly brutal with PNM supporters looting Indian shops and homes while the predominantly black police made house by house searches for arms in Indian areas. Rudranath foolishly declared the Indians would overthrow the government by force but did nothing. Williams declared a state of emergency. Rudranath broke down and returned to England where he lived in Brighton. Gomes also soon fled.[50]

Appendix B
Naipaul, Trinidad and Africa

As some critics interpret Naipaul's writings as prejudiced against blacks or the third world, a summary of a few additional facts about the racial politics of Trinidad may be useful. Trinidad and Guyana are among the new nations whose populations are not native and where the coming of independence created mutual fears of dominance between opposing ethnic groups. The period between 1946 and 1961 was particularly bad in Trinidad as the black urban population, led by Eric Williams, was pressing for complete independence from England and for a Trinidadian-led Caribbean Federation, while the Indian population opposed both, fearing domination by black majorities. Eric Williams, who led the People's National Movement, was charismatic, tough, unscrupulous and influenced by the Marxist model of a one-party state. Having led Trinidad towards independence he believed opposition was treasonable. Although he spoke of the need for a multiracial Trinidad he used a rhetoric of religious deliverance in which national freedom meant government by those of African descent. When in power he appointed no Hindu Indians to the senior positions and, according to C. L. R. James, some of the leadership of Williams' People's National Movement were fanatically anti-Hindu Indian (although the PNM did include Moslem Indians).[51] The violence and accusations of treason against Indians during the period 1946 to 1961 undoubtedly influenced Naipaul's view of decolonization in unhomogeneous, mixed societies, a view that would have been reinforced by the confiscation of the businesses and the expulsions of Indians from newly independent East and Central African nations. The same liberal politicians and intellectuals who in Europe and the United States favoured independence

156

and black rule in Africa and the Caribbean seldom spoke up
against the mistreatment of Indians, and sometimes justified it by
arguing that the Indians were an alien entrepreneurial class who
blocked black advancement into business. (Notice the comments
of Linda and Bobby about Indian shopkeepers in 'In a Free State'.)
Considering Naipaul's experience in Trinidad and his observations of Guyana and Africa he seems surprisingly analytical about
the causes of black discrimination against Indians; he distinguishes
between nations, such as the United States and England, where
those of African descent are a minority subject to discrimination
and nations where they discriminate against others or, as in parts
of Africa, among themselves. Those who believe that all post-
colonial literature consists of resistance to imperialist, capitalist,
white patriarchy might remember that post-structuralism is founded
on '*différance*' and that deconstruction aims at demythification of
stereotypes.

Notes

1. Many of Naipaul's sources and allusions are mentioned in John Thieme, *The Web of Allusions* (London: Hansib, 1988).
2. The factual basis of many of the writings can be found in Landeg White, *V. S. Naipaul* (London: Macmillan, 1975).
3. Rhonda Cobham, 'The *Caribbean Voices* Programme and the Development of West Indian Short Fiction: 1945–1958' in Peter O. Stummer (ed.), *The Story Must Be Told: Short Narrative Prose in the New English Literature* (Würzburg: Konigshausen & Neuman, 1986), pp. 146–60.
4. V. S. Naipaul, 'Our Universal Civilization', *The New York Review of Books* (31 January 1991), 22–5.
5. See Ben Whitaker (ed.), *The Fourth World: Victims of Group Oppression* (New York: Schocken, 1973). The situation for Indians became worse in Uganda and Zaire.
6. It was not just Williams. Arnold Rampersad remembers 'the ever-present campaign of humiliation and demoralization and threats of violence aimed at Indians . . . in the capital, Port of Spain, in the late 1940s. . . . I do not want to leave the impression that East Indians were not, for their part, hostile to Afro-Trinidadians. However, they were a minority, and their normal hostility took a different, far less physical form, and counted for almost nothing in Port of Spain, where few Indians lived.' Rampersad says, 'it is no more possible to understand Naipaul's mind and art without reference to racism, violence, and intolerance in Trinidad than to understand Richard Wright without reference to the same factors in the South.' He sees both as exiles wounded by their 'homes', who turned to travel writing. Arnold Rampersad, 'V. S. Naipaul: Turning in the South', *Raritan*, 20:1 (Summer 1990), 24–47: 45–6.
7. See Bruce King (ed.), *West Indian Literature* (London: Macmillan, 1979), and Kenneth Ramchand, *The West Indian Novel and its Background* (London: Faber, 1970).
8. See Naipaul's 'Foreword' to *The Adventures of Gurudeva and Other Stories* (London: Deutsch, 1976); and Reinhard W. Sander, *The Trinidad Awakening: West Indian Literature of the Nineteen-Thirties* (New York: Greenwood Press, 1988), p. 150.
9. *The Adventures*, pp. 9–10.
10. Bill Ashcroft, Gareth Griffiths and Helen Tiffin, *The Empire Writes Back: Theory and Practice in Post-Colonial Literatures* (London: Routledge, 1989), pp. 88–91.
11. Landeg White, *V. S. Naipaul* (London: Macmillan, 1975), p. 50.
12. Ivar Oxaal, *Black Intellectuals Come to Power: The Rise of Creole Nationalism in Trinidad and Tobago* (Cambridge, Mass.: Schenkman, 1968), pp. 100–1. As late as 1961 PNM posters described Eric Williams as

'Moses II'. The use of Messianic rhetoric was earlier associated with Uriah Butler.

13. Earl Lovelace, *The Dragon Can't Dance* (Burnt Mill, Harlow: Longman Caribbean Writers Series, 1986; first published 1979), p. 23.

14. Oxaal's *Black Intellectuals Come to Power* is useful for the Capildeos. See pp. 160–80.

15. George Lamming also sees the West Indian black community both as absurdly mimicking the English and as overly racially sensitive. See Lamming, 'A Wedding in the Spring', *Commonwealth Short Stories*, ed. Anna Rutherford and Donald Hannah (London: Edward Arnold, 1971; Macmillan, 1979), pp. 44–56.

16. The People's National Movement was led by Dr Eric Williams and the Democratic Labour Party had Dr Rudranath Capildeo as its leader although, unlike Williams, his scholarship and display of knowledge had no political direction.

17. See Selwyn D. Ryan, *Race and Nationalism in Trinidad and Tobago* (University of Toronto Press, 1972), pp. 146–7 and p. 157.

18. 'Unaccommodated man is no more but such a poor, bare, forked animal as thou art' (*King Lear*, III.iv). 'Nothing will come of nothing' (*Lear*, I.i). When Anand sees a lamp during the storm the allusion is to *Lear*, III.4, when Gloucester enters with a torch: 'Look, here comes a walking fire'.

19. See the discussion in the books by Thieme and Boxill listed in the Bibliography. Also see Geoffrey Riley, 'Echoes of Wells in Naipaul's *A House for Mr Biswas*', *Notes and Queries*, 36 (234): 2 (June 1989), 208–9.

20. Bruce King, 'Anand's Recherche du Temps Perdu', *Commonwealth*, 6, No. 1 (Autumn 1983), 1–18.

21. Naipaul's use of H. G. Wells' Mr Polly has been discussed by, among others, Anthony Boxill, *V. S. Naipaul's Fiction: In Quest of the Enemy* (Fredericton, New Brunswick: York Press, 1983).

22. See Richard Cronin, *Imagining India* (New York: St. Martin's Press, 1989).

23. I have discussed this paradox in Bruce King, *The New English Literature: Cultural nationalism in a changing world* (London, Macmillan, 1980).

24. See Gordon Rohlehr, 'Talking about Naipaul', *Carib*, No. 2 (1981), 39–65, esp. 49–52.

25. See James Pollack, 'The Parenthetic Destruction of Metaphor in V. S. Naipaul's *The Mimic Men*'. *Osmania Journal of English Studies* (December 1982) 90–9 (V. S. Naipaul Special Number).

26. V. S. Naipaul, 'The Documentary Heresy', *20th Century*, 173 (Winter 1964–5), 107–8.

27. Eric Roach, 'Fame a Short-lived Cycle, says Vidia', *Trinidad Guardian*, 4 January 1972, p. 1.

28. Singh's Roman House may ironically allude to Eric Williams' house on Lady Chancellor's Road where the founding members of the PNM met.

29. See *India: A Wounded Civilization*, pp. 18–27, 37–43.

30. Vivek Dhareshwar, 'Self-fashioning, Colonial Habitus, and Double Exclusion: V. S. Naipaul's *The Mimic Men*', *Criticism* 31:1 (Winter 1989), 75–102.

31. Nan Doerksen, '*In A Free State* and *Nausea*', *World Literature Written in English*, 20: 1 (Spring 1981), 101–13.
32. U. R. Anantha Murthy, *Samskara: A Rite for a Dead Man*, translated by A. K. Ramanujan (Delhi: Oxford University Press, 1976). Naipaul discusses this novel in *India: A Wounded Civilization*, pp. 104–12.
33. M. Banning Eyre, 'Naipaul at Wesleyan', *The South Carolina Review*, 14 (Spring 1982), 34–47: 45.
34. Bharati Mukherjee and Robert Boyers, 'A Conversation with V. S. Naipaul', *Salmagundi*, 54 (Fall 1981), 4–22: 16.
35. Harold Barratt, 'In Defence of Naipaul's *Guerrillas*', *World Literature Written in English*, 28:1 (1988), 97–103.
36. Ivar Oxaal, *Race and Revolutionary Consciousness: A Documentary Interpretation of the 1970 Black Power Revolt in Trinidad* (Cambridge, Mass: Schenkman, 1971).
37. Cathleen Medwick, 'Life, literature, and politics: an interview with V. S. Naipaul', *Vogue*, August 1981, pp. 129–30: 130.
38. V. S. Naipaul, 'Without a Dog's Chance', *The New York Review of Books*, 18 (18 May 1972), 29–31.
39. Quoted by Farrukh Dhondy in Lisa Appignanesi and Sara Maitland (eds), *The Rushdie File* (Syracuse: Syracuse University Press, 1990), p. 184.
40. See Ivar Oxaal, *Black Intellectuals Come to Power: The Rise of Creole Nationalism* (Cambridge, Mass.: Schenkman, 1968), pp. 100–1.
41. V. S. Naipaul interviewed by Adrian Rowe-Evans, *Transition*, 40 (1971), 56–62: 57, 58.
42. V. S. Naipaul, 'A Plea for Rationality', *Indians in the Caribbean*, ed. I. J. Bahadur Singh (New Delhi: Sterling, 1987), pp. 17–30: 27.
43. See Naipaul's comments about Islamic historiography in his 'Our Universal Civilization', *The New York Review of Books* (31 January 1991), 22–5.
44. Some of the European classical sources are discussed in Steven Blakemore, '"An Africa of Words": V. S. Naipaul's *A Bend in the River*', *The South Carolina Review*, 18:1 (Fall 1985), 15–23.
45. Michael Neill, 'Guerrillas and Gangs: Frantz Fanon and V. S. Naipaul', *Ariel*, 13:4 (1982), 21–62: see 43–5.
46. M. Banning Eyre, 'Naipaul at Wesleyan', *The South Carolina Review* (Spring 1982), 34–47: 46.
47. I discuss Greene's use of Dante in 'Graham Greene's Inferno', *Etudes Anglaises*, 21:1 (1968), 35–51.
48. V. S. Naipaul, 'Argentina: Living with Cruelty', *The New York Review of Books;* 39, No. 3 (30 January 1992), 13.
49. As there is no bend in the Ganges in the classical Sanskrit texts of *Ramayana*, I wrote to ask Naipaul if he had a different version in mind. He replied that he was struck by the title of Malgonkar's novel.
50. Appendix A is based on the books by Landeg White, Scott MacDonald and Ivar Oxaal (*Black Intellectuals Come to Power*) listed in the Bibliography. See MacDonald, pp. 119–20, 135. Also see Brinsley Samaroo, 'Politics and Afro-Indian Relations in Trinidad', in John La Guerre (ed), *Calcutta to Caroni* (Longman Caribbean, 1974), pp. 84–97.
51. See Selwyn D. Ryan, *Race and Nationalism in Trinidad and Tobago* (University of Toronto Press, 1972), p. 201.

Selected Bibliography

BOOKS BY V. S. NAIPAUL

Dates are of first publication; page references are to Penguin editions, first date of publication ( ).

The Mystic Masseur, 1957 (1964).
The Suffrage of Elvira, 1958 (1969).
Miguel Street, 1959 (1971).
A House for Mr Biswas, 1961; with a 'Foreword', 1983 (1969).
The Middle Passage: Impressions of Five Societies, 1962 (1969).
Mr Stone and the Knights Companion, 1963 (1969).
An Area of Darkness: An Experience of India, 1964 (1968).
The Mimic Men, 1967 (1969).
A Flag on the Island, 1968 (1969).
The Loss of El Dorado: A History, 1969; revised edition, 1973 (1973).
In a Free State, 1971 (1973).
The Overcrowded Barracoon and Other Articles, 1972 (1976).
Guerrillas, 1975 (1976).
India: A Wounded Civilization, 1977 (1979).
A Bend in the River, 1979 (1980).
'The Return of Eva Perón' with 'The Killings in Trinidad', 1980 (1981).
A Congo Diary (Los Angeles: Sylvester & Orphanpos), 1980.
Among the Believers: An Islamic Journey, 1981 (1982).
Finding the Centre: Two Narratives, 1984 (1985).
The Enigma of Arrival, 1987 (1987).
A Turn in the South, 1989 (1989).
India: A Million Mutinies, 1990.

OTHER WRITINGS BY NAIPAUL

'Critics and Criticism', *Bim*, 10:38 (January–June 1964), 74–7.
'The Documentary Heresy', *20th Century*, 173 (Winter 1964–5), 107–8.
'Foreword', in *The Adventures of Gurudeva and Other Stories* by Seepersad Naipaul (London: André Deutsch, 1976).
'On Being a Writer', *The New York Review of Books* (23 April 1987), 7.
'Our Universal Civilization', *The New York Review of Books* (31 January 1991), 22–5.
'A Plea for Rationality', in *Indians in the Caribbean*, ed. I. J. Bahadur Singh (New Delhi: Sterling, 1987), pp. 17–30.

161

162   *V. S. Naipaul*

'Without a Dog's Chance', *The New York Review of Books* (18 May 1972), 29–31.
'Argentina: Living with Cruelty', *The New York Review of Books*, 39, No. 3 (30 January 1992), 13–18.

INTERVIEWS

James Applewhite, 'A Trip with V. S. Naipaul', *Raritan*, 10:1 (Summer 1990), 48–54.

Nigel Bingham, 'The Novelist V. S. Naipaul Talks about his Childhood', *The Listener*, 7 September 1972, pp. 306–67.

M. Banning Eyre, 'Naipaul at Wesleyan', *The South Carolina Review*, 14 (Spring 1982), 34–47.

Elizabeth Hardwick, 'Meeting V. S. Naipaul', *New York Times Book Review* (13 May 1979), 1, 36.

Michael Harris, 'Naipaul on Campus: Sending out a Plea for Rationality', *Tapia* [Trinidad] (29 June 1975), 2.

Alfred Kazin, ' V. S. Naipaul, Novelist as Thinker', *The New York Review of Books* (1 May 1977), 20–1.

Cathleen Medwick, 'Life, literature, and politics: an interview with V. S. Naipaul', *Vogue*, August 1981, pp. 129–30.

Charles Michener, 'The Dark Visions of V. S. Naipaul', *Newsweek*, 16 November 1981, pp. 104–17.

Bharati Mukherjee and Robert Boyers, 'A Conversation with V. S. Naipaul', *Salmagundi*, 54 (1981), 4–22.

Eric Roach, 'Fame a Short-lived Cycle, says Vidia', *Trinidad Guardian*, 4 January 1972, pp. 1–2.

Adrian Rowe-Evans, 'V. S. Naipaul', *Transition* [Ghana], 40 (1971), 56–62.

Derek Walcott, 'Interview with V. S. Naipaul', *Sunday Guardian* [Trinidad], 7 March 1965, pp. 5, 7.

SECONDARY READINGS

General Background

Bill Ashcroft, Gareth Griffiths and Helen Tiffin, *The Empire Writes Back: Theory and Practice in Post-colonial Literatures* (London: Routledge, 1989).

David Dabydeen and Brinsley Samaroo (eds), *India in the Caribbean* (London: Hansib Publishing, 1988).

Bruce King, *The New English Literatures: Cultural nationalism in a changing world* (London: Macmillan, 1980).

Bruce King (ed.), *West Indian Literature* (London: Macmillan 1979).

Morton Klass, *East Indians in Trinidad* (London: Columbia University Press, 1961).

John La Guerre (ed.), *Calcutta to Caroni: The East Indians of Trinidad* (London: Longman, 1974).

David Lowenthal, *West Indian Societies* (London: Oxford University Press, 1972).

Scott B. MacDonald, *Trinidad and Tobago: Democracy and Development in the Carribean* (New York; Praeger, 1986).

Yogendra Malik, *East Indians in Trinidad: A Study in Minority Politics* (London: Oxford University Press, 1971).

Seepersad Naipaul, *Gurudeva and Other Indian Tales* (Port of Spain: Trinidad Publishers, 1943).

Ivar Oxaal, *Black Intellectuals Come to Power: The Rise of Creole Nationalism in Trinidad & Tobago* (Cambridge, Mass: Schenkman, 1968).

Ivar Oxaal, *Race and Revolutionary Consciousness: A Documentary Interpretation of the 1970 Black Power Revolt in Trinidad* (Cambridge, Mass.: Schenkman, 1971).

Kenneth Ramchand, *The West Indian Novel and Its Background* (London: Heinemann Educational, 2nd edn, 1984).

Selwyn D. Ryan, *Race and Nationalism in Trinidad and Tobago: A Study of decolonization in a multiracial society* (Toronto: University of Toronto Press, 1972).

Reinhard W. Sander, *The Trinidad Awakening: West Indian Literature of the Nineteen-Thirties* (New York: Greenwood Press, 1988).

Ben Whitaker (ed.), *The Fourth World: Victims of Group Oppression* (New York: Schocken Books, 1973).

SOME BOOKS ABOUT NAIPAUL

Anthony Boxill, *V. S. Naipaul's Fiction: In Quest of the Enemy* (Fredericton, New Brunswick: York Press, 1983).

Robert Hamner, *V. S. Naipaul* (New York: Twayne, 1973).

Robert Hamner (ed.), *Critical Perspectives on V. S. Naipaul* (Washington, DC: Three Continents Press, 1977).

Dolly Zulakha Hassan, *V. S. Naipaul and the West Indies* (New York: Peter Lang, 1989).

Kelvin Jarvis, *V. S. Naipaul: A Selective Bibliography with Annotations, 1957–1987* (Metuchen, New Jersey: Scarecrow, 1989).

Robert K. Morris, *Paradoxes of Order: Some Perspectives on the Fiction of V. S. Naipaul* (Columbia: University of Missouri, 1975).

Peggy Nightingale, *Journey Through Darkness: The Writing of V. S. Naipaul* (St Lucia: University of Queensland Press, 1987).

Paul Theroux, *V. S. Naipaul: An Introduction to His Work* (London: André Deutsch, 1972).

John Thieme, *The Web of Tradition: Uses of Allusion in V. S. Naipaul's Fiction* (London: Hansib Publishing, 1988).

Landeg White, *V. S. Naipaul* (London: Macmillan, 1975).

SPECIAL ISSUES OF JOURNALS

Commonwealth, 6, No. 1 (Autumn 1983).

Commonwealth, 9, No. 1 (Autumn 1986).

Modern Fiction Studies, 30, No. 3 (Autumn 1984).

Osmania Journal of English Studies, V. S. Naipaul Special Number (December 1982).

ARTICLES

Harold Barratt, 'In Defence of Naipaul's *Guerrillas*', *World Literature Written in English*, 28:1 (Spring 1988), 97–101.

Steven Blakemore, '"An Africa of Words": V. S. Naipaul's *A Bend in the River*', *South Carolina Review*, 18:1 (Fall 1985), 15–23.

John Carthew, 'Adapting to Trinidad: Mr Biswas and Mr Polly Revisited', *Journal of Commonwealth Literature*, 13: 1 (1978), 58–64.

Rhonda Cobham, 'The *Caribbean Voices* Programme and the Development of West Indian Short Fiction: 1945–1958' in *The Story Must Be Told: Short Narrative Prose in the New English Literatures*, ed. Peter O. Stummer (Würzburg: Konigshausen & Neumann, 1986), pp. 146–60.

Richard Cronin, '*An Area of Darkness*' in *Imagining India* (New York: St. Martin's Press, 1989), pp. 103–13.

Vivek Dhareshwar, 'Self-fashioning, Colonial Habitus, and Double Exclusion: V. S. Naipaul's *The Mimic Men*', *Criticism*, 31:I (Winter 1989), 75–102.

Nan Doerksen, '*In a Free State* and *Nausea*', *World Literature Written in English*, 20 (1981), 105–13.

Joseph Epstein, 'A Cottage for Mr Naipaul', *The New Criterion*, 6:2 (October 1987), 6–15.

Michel Fabre, 'By Words Possessed: The Education of Mr Biswas as a Writer', *Commonwealth Essays and Studies* (Dijon), 9:1 (Autumn 1986), 59–61.

Martin Fido, 'A Bend in the River', *Bim*, 17: 66–7 (June 1983), 129–32.

Graham Huggan, 'Anxieties of Influence: Conrad in the Caribbean', *Commonwealth*, 11:1 (Autumn 1988), 1–12.

Trevor Ludema, 'Defending CLR James', *Trinidad Guardian*, 1 November 1970, p. 5.

Gloria Lynn, 'A Thing Called Art: The Mimic Men', *Carib*, No. 2 (1981), 66–77.

Bruce MacDonald, 'The Birth of Mr Biswas', *Journal of Commonwealth Literature*, 11:3 (1977), 50–4.

Melina Nathan, 'V. S. Naipaul's The Enigma of Arrival', *New Voices* [Trinidad] 18:35/36 (March–September 1990), 43–67.

Michael Neill, 'Guerrillas and the Gangs: Frantz Fanon and V. S. Naipaul', *Ariel*, 13:4 (1982), 21–62.

Kenneth Ramchand, 'A House for Mr Biswas', *An Introduction to the Study of West Indian Literature* (Kingston: Nelson Caribbean, 1976), pp. 73–90.

Arnold Rampersad, 'V. S. Naipaul: Turning in the South', *Raritan*, 10.1 (Summer 1990), 24–39.

Victor J. Ramraj, 'V. S. Naipaul: The Irrelevance of Nationalism', *World Literature Written in English*, 23:1 (Winter 1984), 187–96.

Geoffrey Riley, 'Echoes of Wells in Naipaul's *A House for Mr Biswas*', *Notes and Queries*, 36 (234):2 (June 1989), 208–9.

Gordon Rohlehr [interviewed by Selwyn Cudjoe], 'Talking about Naipaul', *Carib*, No. 2 (1981), 39–65.

Richard I. Smyer, 'Naipaul's *A Bend in the River*: Fiction and the Post-colonial Tropics', *The Literary Half-Yearly*, 25:1 (January 1984), 55–65.

Sara Suleri, 'Naipaul's Arrival', *The Yale Journal of Criticism*, 2:1 (Fall 1988), 25–50.

Thorell Tsomondo, 'Metaphor, Metonymy and Houses: Figures of Construction in *A House for Mr Biswas*', *World Literature Written in English*, 29:2 (Autumn 1989), 69–82.

Derek Walcott, 'The Achievement of V. S. Naipaul', *Sunday Guardian* [Trinidad], 12 April 1964, p. 15.

Derek Walcott, 'The Garden Path', *The New Republic*, 13 April 1987, pp. 27–31.

Index